Arthur! Arthur!

More Comic Sketches from the Master's Pen

ARTHUR BLACK

Stoddart

To glorious, beleaguered, raggedy-assed CBC Radio — the best thing anybody ever stuck in Canada's ear

Copyright © 1991 by Arthur Black

First published in 1991 by
Stoddart Publishing Co. Limited
34 Lesmill Road
Toronto, Canada
M3B 2T6

Canadian Cataloguing in Publication Data

Black, Arthur
  Arthur! Arthur!

ISBN 0-7737-2513-X

I. Title.

PS8553.L33A77 1991   C814'.54   C91-094815-1
PR9199.3.B53A77 1991

Some of these sketches have been broadcast on CBC Radio or have appeared in the pages of various newspapers across the country. Many thanks to the CBC and to the relevant editors and publishers for permission to have them reappear in ARTHUR! ARTHUR!

Cover Design: Brant Cowie/Art Plus Limited
Typesetting: Tony Gordon Ltd.

Printed and bound in the United States of America

Contents

PART 1
Who We Are

O Cana-a-do (re, mi)

WANNA WIN A BAR bet? I'll tell ya how to win a bar bet. Walk into a bar, pick out the meekest, mildest, most unassuming schmo you can find, sidle up, start a conversation and, when the moment seems appropriate, say: "So . . . what part of the States are ya from?"

He says, "Oh, I'm not American . . . I'm Canadian."

You got 'im.

Just wink, shrug, look away, sip your coffee.

He'll say, "Whassa matter — you don't believe I'm Canadian?"

You say, "Hey, if you say so. None of my business." Sip your coffee.

He gets a little red, says, "I'm Canadian, darn it!" Whips out his driver's licence, his library card, his hospitalization.

You glance at the ID. Whistle. Say, "Good job. Must've cost you a bundle."

He's really red now. He says, "Hey, I'm Canadian — I'll betcha twenty bucks I'm Canadian!"

Now you've really got 'im.

You say, "Okay, if you're Canadian I guess for twenty bucks it would be easy for you to sing the Canadian national anthem."

Money in the bank. There's not a Canuck from Joe Batt's Arm to the Queen Charlottes who can warble "O Canada" at the drop of a double sawback — except for Roger Doucet, and he's dead.

It's not that Canadians are slow learners — we got ourselves a tough anthem to sing, full of glowings and gloriouses and thous and thees. The tune is fine, but the words are a little wheezy. Which is not surprising. The lyrics were penned by a Quebec City lawyer more than a hundred years ago. The full version of "O Canada" includes lines such as "Thou land of hope, for all who toil" and "May stalwart sons and gentle maidens rise." Today, Canadians don't embarrass themselves beyond one mumbling of the first verse and the refrain, but even that's a struggle. "True patriot love . . . in all thy sons command" — does anyone have any idea exactly what that means?

All of which leaves us with what must be a singular phenomenon in the twentieth century: a club of twenty-seven million members who can't sing their own theme song.

But when you think of it — so what? Consider the nationalities that wear their national anthems like tattoos and trumpet them out at the drop of a flag: the French and their "Marseillaise," the British with "God Save the Queen," the Russian "Internationale" and of course the American "Star-Spangled Banner." Rip-roaring tunes, every one of them, but all with an "I'm the King of the Castle" quality to them. As Canadian writer William L. Grant once said, "There are too many nasty little self-centred nations in the world already; God forbid that Canada should add one to the number!"

Something to think about the next time we get to watch lager louts swaying drunkenly to the strains of "God Save the Queen" at a U.K. soccer match. Or American fans in baseball caps holding their paper cups of watery beer at heart level as they sing along with the Jumbotron "What so proudly we hailed . . ."

Something for Canadians to think of, not sing to: maybe we're the kinder gentler nation George Bush has been wistfully dreaming about.

Definition of a Canadian — To Be Announced

STRANGELY INDISTINCT, this country of ours. Say words like Italy, France or America, and images swarm to mind. But Canada? Well, it's not exactly this, but it's a little bit of that. One thing for sure . . . it's not the States, eh?

Canada probably deserves a spot in the *Guinness Book of Records* for the country with the most attempted definitions of itself. Ralph Allan made the case for Canada the Accident, pointing out that it only exists as a nation thanks to the vainglory of the English, the treachery of the French (for abandoning their colonies), the incompetence of the Americans who invaded twice but neglected to stay . . . and the tragedy of the Indians — the virtual extinction of the Hurons, the Iroquois and the Algonquins.

A Quebec publisher once compared Canada to a human hand, with the thumb as the Maritimes, the forefinger as Quebec. The prairies represented the ring finger and the West Coast the little finger. A fairly shaky analogy, though I'm sure he got no quarrel from the other digits over his characterization of Ontario as the middle finger.

All kinds of definitions of Canada . . . Dave Broadfoot says we are a collection of ten provinces loosely connected by fear.

Voltaire dismissed us as a few acres of snow. The English poet Rupert Brooke allowed as how we were "a live country . . . live, but not kicking."

Marshall McLuhan suggested that Canada's identity is the fact that she has no identity. Hmm. Canada as a Void. So it is for some observers.

I still remember the American student being interviewed on a radio show who said, "You never hear anything bad about Canada, that's one thing . . . (pause) . . . In fact, that's the only thing."

Canada as Wallflower? Marilyn Monroe: "When they said Canada, I thought it would be up in the mountains somewhere." Al Capone: "Hey, I don't even know what street Canada's on."

Canada as Concubine? U.S. financier/tycoon J. P. Morgan: "Canada is a very nice place and we're going to keep it that way."

Canada as collapsed soufflé? John Robert Colombo: "Canada could have enjoyed English government, French culture and American know-how. Instead we wound up with French government, English know-how and American culture."

There've been a couple of culinary stabs at defining our homeland. We've been called a Tossed Salad side order to the American Melting Pot. Stuart Keate said we were more like vichyssoise — cold, half French and difficult to stir.

Whatever we are, we've been working at it for a hundred and a quarter years now, and that's worth clinking our glasses. We will celebrate . . . but quietly. The Canadian way. Not like the bash our flashy neighbours throw on July 4. They have skyrockets and streamers and speeches and parades and pompom girls. Americans kick out the jambs for the Glorious Fourth. Up here we observe . . . Canada Day.

Someone once asked Robertson Davies why Canadians didn't — you know — *love* their country the way Americans do. He replied that Canada isn't a country you love. It's a country you worry about.

But let's not worry next Canada Day. Let's just have a party. Let's all try to remember the second verse of "O Canada." Let's dream about what we're going to be when we grow up.

Canucks in the Land of Anita Bryant

M R. BLACK LEANS more towards the Beet-Red end of the colour spectrum this week. Beet red because last week, while hi-ho-ing to work along the 401, past the Hydra-runwayed monster that is Lester B. Pearson International, fishbelly-white Black did an uncharacteristic thing. He followed the little green-and-white airplane symbols, abandoned his snow-caked clunker to the mercies of Park 'n' Fly and climbed aboard Eastern Airlines flight 785 to Fort Myers, Florida.

Audacious? Hardly. I was but one of a million and a half snow-weary Canadians who at some point each winter straggle down the Eastern Seaboard to fight for roosting space on that stubby stump of the continent that juts into the Caribbean.

Each year we pump some two billion Canadian dollars into the Florida economy. That's enough money that, were we all to decide to stay home one year and tend to our driveways, we would wipe out the Canadian tourism deficit at a stroke.

We leave a lot of money down there. But we leave our mark, too. There's a weekly newspaper in Florida called *Canada News*, circulation 7,000. There's a radio program carried on twenty-eight Florida stations — a daily digest of Canadian news — with heavy emphasis on blizzards and cold snaps. On the first night in my Florida hotel room I turned on the TV and discovered I could choose from: an hour-long update on the Canadian identity crisis; a documentary on the fate of the Franklin expedition to Canada's Arctic; an NHL hockey game between the Oilers and the Rangers.

I don't know how well Canada is faring elsewhere in the battle to preserve our culture, but in Florida we qualify as Imperialist Warlords.

Still somewhat short of Attila the Hun, however. Canadians in Florida are if anything more diffident and polite than they are at home. It's easy to spot Canadians in Florida. Their distinctive calls are the plaintive "Excuse me?" and "Thank you." You can always tell when the snowbirds are nesting in a flock of Sunshine Staters, too. There's a kind of avian call-and-response litany between Canadians and Floridians that goes: "Thank you," "Uh-huh," "Thanks, eh?" "Uh-huh."

But there's something about Canucks, even in Florida. I sat in on a convention of Canadian contractors while I was down there. The American hosts did it up . . . well, like Americans. They had a live musical trio splayed out under a Stars and Stripes as big as a shopping mall awning, just to play and sing the national anthems to open the proceedings. The soloist booms into the first few bars of "O, say can you see . . ." expecting the whole room to thunder along with him. . . . Not a sound. Just 450 Canadians standing respectfully, but silently. They do not sing other countries' anthems. The soloist, clearly flustered, finishes "The Star-Spangled Banner," then, as his partner chords on the piano, announces ruefully, "Well, here's one you can sing along with," and breaks into 'O CAANADAAAA . . .'"

And of course he's wrong. Canadians can't sing their own anthem very well, either. Oh, we stumble along for a verse or so, but then somebody throws in a half-remembered French line and then everybody falters on "All thy sons command" because didn't Ottawa decide that was sexist — or was that a parliamentary subcommittee to rename Dildo, Newfoundland? Aw, it's complicated being a Canadian, that's for sure.

"O Canada" drones on in the convention hall, three, maybe four off-key versions being warbled simultaneously. The American trio by now has no idea what's going on, but it makes a crazy kind of sense to a Canadian. As much sense as a country that is half French and half English, half European and half North American, half in love with the U.S. and half afraid of it, half winter and half summer . . . and in that tremulous halting medley of voices singing a song that never soars, but never stops, there is a curious kind of quintessentially Canadian strength. And I can't help thinking that if as a nation we sang better, we might fare worse.

Is that contradictory? Well, that's Canadian, too, eh?

Canada Beneath the Blankets

THERE'S GOOD NEWS and there's bad news today. The bad news is that pollsters are back in the news; the good news is the pollsters have nothing to do with statistical assessments of your local town council, the provincial legislature or Parliament Hill. The pollsters in the news are not polling about politics . . . they're polling about love. Canadian style.

I dunno if it's coincidence or the impending visit of Saint Valentine and all the loopy midwinter goofiness that day inspires . . . but for some reason the soothsayers at Gallup and the entrail readers at Decima Research have been poring over the phenomenon of love and romance as they're practised in the Great White North . . . and they've stumbled across some pretty interesting findings.

According to Decima, Newfoundland wins the red garter for most amorous province in Confederation. Seventy-seven per cent of Newfoundlanders enthusiastically rate themselves as "sexually active." That's nearly 10 per cent above the national average.

But what's this? Here's some exhausted Gallup pollsters weighing in with results from the West Coast. B.C. is where the action is, says Gallup. According to their surveys, 93 per cent of British Columbians over the age of eighteen have been around the bases, compared with a paltry 81 per cent of Maritimers. A Gallup vice-president went so far as to dub British Columbia "The Babylon of Canada."

Well, 93 per cent in the West, 81 per cent in the East . . . Ganges or Gander, Kitimat or Carbonear, the oversexed headboard and footboard of this country seem to be in fine fettle. What I want to know is, what about the rest of us in the middle? You prairie farmers. The wheat's all in . . . you got time on your hands . . . And you, Ontario — c'mon, there's more to life than making money. Quebec. Quebec? You awake?

But then Love Canadian Style has always been a bewildering business at best. A few years ago one of this country's most famous satyrs, Irving Layton, wondered why it was that a stuffy Frigidaire of a country like Canada could turn out some of the best love poetry in the world.

Layton concluded it was because, as he put it, "Canadians are a backward folk; they have not yet heard that love is dead." Adventurous folk, too. John Kenneth Galbraith, the world-famous economist and pundit, recalls his teenage years in Southwestern Ontario lust thusly:

"In winter, a cutter lent itself to lovemaking only at the cost of extreme contortion and an occasional chilling exposure. The alternative was a snowbank. Things were not appreciably more agreeable in the autumn on the frozen ground, in the spring in the mud, or in summer under the onslaught of the mosquitos. Chastity was everywhere protected by a vigilant nature."

Vigilant, but not unbreachable. Pierre Berton defines a Canadian as someone who knows how to make love in a canoe. That's what it takes to be a citizen in a country of great lovers, I guess — a certain backwardness, a sense of adventure and above all resourcefulness. Nobody puts it more pithily than Marie Lynne Hammond who sings, "Canadian love, Canadian love . . . it's forty below or it's ninety above."

Won't be ninety above for a while yet, so stay warm, folks. And don't get distracted by a knock on the door. It's probably just a nosey pollster.

Hey, Big Boy—
Got a Macho?

L ET US PAUSE for a moment's respectful silence on behalf of Australian manhood. The second shoe has dropped.

The first shoe was a dusty cowboy boot and it covered the foot of a character called Crocodile Dundee. You remember Crocodile . . . a lean and rangy chap with an easygoing smile and a pocket knife big enough to shishkebab a sperm whale on.

Actor Paul Hogan portrayed the wily outbacker in two movies that injected hundreds of millions of dollars into the Australian economy and put the land Down Under on the map. Now everybody in the whole world knows what Australian men are like. They're cuddly, they're fearless, they wear hats festooned with crocodile teeth and they get the girl in the end.

Nope. That's what I meant about the other shoe dropping. Psychologists, writers and other surveyors of the passing scene are now emerging from the woodwork to tell the world that Crocodile Dundee is a myth.

"Australian males may think themselves tough, wily and worldly like Dundee," says Australian writer Berwyn Lewis, "but most are benignly adolescent . . . products of a country that has never suffered a revolution, a civil war or a saturation bombing to really test its manhood."

Whatever you think of his yardsticks for masculinity, the man has a point. Australian males are living dangerously over the mythological line. They may see themselves as bare-handed jungle croc wrestlers, but eight out of ten Australians live safely under the streetlights in large cities clustered along the country's coastline. Most of them go home to ranch-style bungalows on postage-

11

stamp lots in suburbs. They bring home paycheques from white collar, soft-pinkie jobs in sales-related service industries. A majority of them couldn't tell a wild crocodile from John Crosbie. The most dangerous thing your average Aussie faces is a beer cap scrape from his Fosters Lager or a flash burn from the "barbie."

But Australian men aren't the only ones who like to dress up their mental image. I had a couple of hours to kill in Cleveland one time, and the only movie house I could find was showing *Rambo* (I forget which number, but it doesn't really matter). On the screen, Rambo had just destroyed two regiments of crack enemy troops, which prompted a blood-curdling cheer from the throats of a dozen cinema patrons seated behind me. I turned around fearfully, expecting to see a couple of rows of neolithic bikers in tattoos, torn T-shirts and chains.

What did I see?

Geeks. Nerds. Skinny little guys with pasty faces and pencil necks, receding hairlines and Coke-bottle-bottom specs.

These were the Americans who were identifying with the superhuman muscle-popping Rambo persona up on the screen — goofy, slope-shouldered misfits with sunken chests and pot bellies who'd come down with angina attacks if they trotted up a flight of stairs. Unathletic guys. Unaggressive guys. Guys like . . .

Well, you and me, I guess.

Which brings it home to Canada. We Canucks have our mythological male, too. He doesn't pack a broadsword-size hunting knife like Crocodile Dundee, and he's not much for state-of-the-art machine guns like Rambo, but he's pretty good with an axe, as long as he faces nothing more hostile than a jack pine. Give him a birchbark canoe and a good stretch of white water and he'll make that paddle sing.

Ah yes, the famous Canadian lumberjack. I confess, I've done my bit to spread the myth. Last winter in Georgia over a mint julep or two I entertained some locals with stories of a typical Canadian lumberjack's life. I told them about our annual bareback moose-riding festivals and the polar-bear-wrestling contests. I believe I even sang a verse or two of "Rose Marie." Just got a card from them — they're coming up for a visit next month. They hope I can take them fishing "for some of those twelve-foot muskies y'all told us about."

Let's see now . . . a canoe is the one with two pointy ends, right?

Canada Annexed.
Film at Eleven

I'VE DONE A FAIR BIT of travelling across this country of ours in the past year. I've visited places as various as Saltspring Island, B.C., and Fredericton, N.B. I've been north as far as Yellowknife and south to Point Pelee. In between I've popped up at Banff and Jasper, Ottawa and Montreal.

Seeing that much national real estate in a relatively short period of time is probably not good for a citizen's perspective. It seduces a guy into issuing pompous generalizations and grand overviews that begin with phrases like "Well, the way I see this country . . ."

Here is my pompous generalizing grand overview: I believe I know what it is that Holds This Nation Together.

It's not the Canadian Broadcasting Corporation and it's not Via Rail (just as well, considering the demolition job the Tory wrecking crews are doing on what's left of those institutions).

It's not professional hockey or Anne Murray that weaves the national fabric together. Neither is it the McKenzie Brothers, nor our habit of hitching the linguistic caboose "eh?" on to everything we say.

It isn't even the cross-Canada hatred for Toronto.

No, the single element that galvanizes this country into an entity, the one constant that pops up everywhere — from office towers on Bay Street to The Yellowknife Inn on the shores of Great Slave Lake. The one thing that holds this country together is . . .

Detroit.

No, I'm serious. Detroit television programming is bombarding Canada and leaving cultural shell holes in places that are thousands of miles beyond that city's limits. You can watch Detroit news shows in Aklavik and Inuvik, in North Bay and Whitehorse. Kids in Thunder Bay and Atikokan are getting the Detroit murder count every night on the six o'clock news. It's all because of the CAN CON satellite service, which picks up the television signals from the three big Detroit TV stations and relays them into cable systems right across our country.

I don't know what CAN CON stands for, but it sure as hell isn't Canadian Content. The stuff that spews out of Detroit, through the television and into Canadian brains consists of American game shows, witless American sitcoms and news and sports reports that are so Detroit oriented that even a Canuck in Windsor would feel left out.

What's wrong with this picture? Plenty. For one thing a whole generation of Canadians — particularly those who live in remote areas without access to other channels — is wired into one of the sleaziest metropolises this continent can dish up. Detroit is over-crowded, gang ridden and slum infested. More people shoot each other in Detroit every year than anywhere else in North America. That's why they call it Murder City. All this is reflected in the Detroit news shows every evening, which often sound more like war-zone body counts than news reports.

Not exactly a superb urban example for Canadian youth.

But even if Detroit was squeaky clean like "Sesame Street," it still wouldn't make it right. Our kids stand a good chance of growing up knowing a lot more about Pontiac and Saginaw than they do about St. John's and Vancouver.

Which may come in handy. According to a recent survey, most Americans would love to make Canada the fifty-first state.

Well, I guess they would.

I'm certain U.S. country singer Lee Greenwood would show us to a chair around the U.S. potbelly stove. He loves Canada — even wrote us a song called "God Bless Canada."

Well . . . sorta wrote us a song. Actually it's his old hit "God Bless the U.S.A." with U.S.A. scratched out and Canada pencilled in. Mind you, he did rewrite one whole verse — which includes the line "From Detroit we can see her/Above the U.S.A. . . ."

Think there'll be jobs for all of us at the Ford plant?

Canadian Passion Not Flagging

YOU KNOW ONE big difference between Americans and Canadians? Flags. They wave 'em; we don't. I'm not sure if it was the lines from that famous poem "Shoot, if you must, this old gray head, but spare your country's flag" . . . or the heroic imagery stirred up in that bombastic old anthem that begins "Oh, say can you see . . ." But something in their culture turned the Americans into rabid standard flappers. They fly flags from their gas stations and their shopping malls. They stick flag decals on their windshields and storm doors. Even the flags on their rural mailboxes are often miniature Stars and Stripes. And whenever there's a parade in the U.S., be it the Rose Bowl or the local chapter of Weight Watchers of America, what's every second person on the sidewalk waving feverishly? An eensy weensy paper version of Old Glory on a stick.

Americans are proud of their flag. Some would suggest excessively so. Canadians? Well, that's a different story.

We have a different flag history in this country. Up until a quarter of a century ago we didn't even have one we could really call our own. We'd gone from the Union Jack to the Red Ensign to, finally, the Maple Leaf on February 15, 1965. Maybe by then Canada was too middle-aged to have a passionate affair with a piece of bunting. Whatever the reason, one of the easiest ways to distinguish a Canadian from an American is to hand each of them his country's flag. The American will look for a strong stick to tie it to and a high hill to fly it from. The Canadian will probably look vaguely embarrassed, fold it neatly and place it at the bottom of a cedar chest.

Doug and Joan Elvy know all about that. The Elvys are untypical Canadians. They are unabashed flag wavers. When they moved into their brand-new home in Kitchener, Ontario, not long ago, one of the first things they did was to sink a twenty-two-foot aluminum flagpole in their backyard and run up a brand-spanking-new, government-issue Maple Leaf flag.

The Elvys thought it looked pretty darned good up there, crackling and snapping in the wind. They thought that until they got the letter from Trillium Estates Limited. Trillium Estates is the corporation that developed the whole area that the Elvys' home is in. The letter, after some bureaucratic jabberwocky, read: "We have no record of approval on file for the erection of the flagpole, nor would we have approved one. We therefore ask that you remove the flagpole from the rear yard of your lot."

Record of approval? Is the subdivision that the Elvys live in some kind of high-security military compound? No. Was it the Swastika or the Hammer and Sickle the Elvys were flying in their backyard? No. It was Canada's national flag. As Joan Elvy so eloquently put it, "What's so offensive about flying a flag?"

Well, the truth is, Joan, there's nothing offensive about it. In America. Or Britain. Or France or Zimbabwe or Denmark or Australia.

Only in Canada you say? Pity.

No Nudes Is Good Nudes

YOU READ Ann Landers often? I must confess I don't. She comes on too much like a wisecracking aunt — which I already have three of — but she did something in her column recently that caught my eye. She called up urban police chiefs across the States and asked them a simple question: what would happen in your city to a person who was seen by the police walking naked down the street?

Turns out, not surprisingly I guess, that such a person would be arrested — or taken into custody, as the police like to say. The authorities would be looking for signs of illegal drug use, intoxication or mental illness.

I wish Ann had asked those cops one supplementary: I wish she'd asked what would happen if the urban nudist was not found to be drunk or drugged or deranged? What would happen if the person convinced the arresting officers that it was such a nice day he/she just felt like taking his/her clothes off?

I'm pretty sure that the cops would scoop the jaybird anyway. We aren't too comfortable with the idea of naked bodies in this society. Unless of course they're strippers or movie stars or close personal friends. In some places nakedness is flat-out illegal. In Austin, Texas, appearing nude in public is a Class C Misdemeanor with fines up to $500. In New York State a person who appears nude in public can get up to fifteen days in jail. Of course in New York it is against the law to show a naked mannequin or dress dummy in the window. This in a city that contains Forty-Second Street, where if you hurry you can line up for such movie features as *Naked and Willing* and *Cycle Sluts Take Manhattan*. . . .

Funny, our attitudes to nudity. In his book *Dancing on the Shore*, Harold Horwood writes about canoeing around Nova Scotia's Goat Island and coming upon a group of young campers.

"They looked as if they'd been going nude all summer," he writes, "their bottoms brown as walnuts. . . . Five hundred years ago young Micmacs must have camped here just like this."

Well, sure, but that would be pre-civilized society, wouldn't it? I'm told that Australian aborigines have no guilt or shame about being naked in public. They'd be mortified if strangers ever saw them eating . . . but being naked is fine.

Don't know how we managed to get such a relatively simple state as bareness all swaddled in layers of guilt and shame, but we did a thorough job of making sure that *skin* rhymes with *sin*. Especially we Anglo Saxons. Someone once said the Anglo-Saxon conscience does not prevent the Anglo Saxon from sinning. It merely prevents him from enjoying it.

Where do Canadians line up on the nudity question? Oh, right along the white line, as usual. The second season of a TV series called "He Shoots He Scores" was aired awhile back on CBC — on both the French and English TV networks. Mind you, the one on Say Bay Say was a few seconds longer than the one shown on CBC. The French language episode had a (gasp) semi-nude scene. Corporation Grundys decided that French-speaking Canadians could handle it, but the rest of us weren't quite ready.

Oh, Canada. The only country in the world that can take the problem of naked bodies in public . . . and wrestle it to a bilingual draw.

Keepers Losers

L UCKIEST PERSON I can think of just off the top of my head would probably be a fella by the name of Enlil-Bani. He was chief gardener for a Babylonian king by the name of Erra-Imitti. (You don't have to remember these names, by the way. I'm just throwing them in so you'll know which Babylonian king's gardener I'm talking about.) Anyway, in ancient Babylonia, they had an off-the-wall way of ringing in the New Year. What they would do is pick out some commoner and crown him king for a day. That was the good news. The bad news was that come sundown he was hauled down and sacrificed. Went from Babylonians' King for a Day to Vultures' Flavour of the Month.

Well, one New Year's Eve, King Erra-Imitti looks around for a scapeserf, and gives the kingly nod to aforementioned gardener Enlil-Bani. Old Enlil-Bani puts down his rake and picks up the sceptre. The sun does its usual overhead arc, and it looks like Enlil is well on his way to the King for a Day scrap heap, when an unusual thing happens.

The real king, Erra-Imitti, ups and dies. Before sundown. What's a Babylonian kingdom to do? Well, what they did was worship newly crowned ex-gardener Enlil-Bani until he died in his sleep in the royal chambers twenty-four years later.

I call that lucky.

This other, more recent thing, I'm not so sure about. You read about that armoured truck cruising along an expressway in Toronto when all of a sudden the back door pops open and three bags of money fly out onto the hoods and windshields of homeward-bound traffic? One of the bags burst. Fifties, twenties, tens and fives fluttering all over the pavement. Cars and trucks screech to a halt. One biker slows down, scoops an entire bag and vrooms away. Seventy-five thousand they figure he got, in one fist.

Sounds like a rejected script for an episode of "Chips," but that's not what gets me. What gets me is the *Globe and Mail* headline next morning. "POLICE LOSING FAITH," it reads. Story says that police are losing faith in the honesty of Toronto motorists because only $15,000 of the lost money has been turned in. Are they serious? Can you imagine such a thing in any city other than Toronto? Can you visualize what would happen if bags of money dropped off an armoured car in Los Angeles? Detroit? Rome? New York? If an armoured truck ever started dropping bags of cash on the New York Interstate, the other commuters would be on it like piranha on a fatted calf. They would not only take the money, they would probably eat the tires.

I figure Toronto motorists deserve a plaque for turning in fifteen grand, which they probably could have got away with scot-free. As for the biker and the other drivers who didn't turn in the cash, well, swell . . . they've got the money. But it isn't happy money. They know it isn't theirs, and unless they're really scumballs, they won't have much of a good time with it.

Reminds me of a story about Abe Lincoln. Seems some guy once tried to bribe him. Would lawyer Lincoln take $100 for some special consideration? Lincoln glowered. Two hundred, perhaps? The stone face remained granite. Five hundred? With a roar Lincoln burst from his chair, grabbed the man by the scruff of the neck and threw him into the street. "Dammit, sir," he thundered, "you came too close to my price!" Which I guess is the good news/bad news for all those folks who kept the money from the armoured-car accident.

The good news is they've got the money. The bad news is they know their price.

Canada: A Mare Usque Ad Nauseam

Oh, don't the days seem lank and long
When all goes right and nothing goes wrong
And isn't your life extremely flat
With nothing whatever to grumble at!

THUS THE SONG-AND-DANCE duet of Gilbert and Sullivan made the case against boredom in an operetta called *Princess Ida* a century ago. They were right, of course. Life would be exceedingly tedious if it was perfect, smooth and as featureless as a cue ball — but that doesn't make bores or boredom any easier to stomach.

And it may be my imagination or just creeping senility, but it seems to me there are more boring things around than when I was a tadpole. The Royal Family is boring. All TV is boring. Most movies (and especially the overhyped ones like *Batman*).

And then of course there's politics. You may have trouble believing this, but there was once such a concept as an exciting politician. They came in all stripes — Tommy Douglas, John Diefenbaker, Stephen Lewis, Pierre Trudeau. Today? We're stuck with bloodless automatons like Joe Clark and Michael Wilson, while we listen to the dial-tone drone of Mulroney and the staccato teletype delivery of Jean Chrétien. These guys transform the concept of an exciting politician into an oxymoron.

I could go on and on but that would just be, well, boring. Besides, I don't have to. Alan Caruba has already done it for me. Caruba is a fifty-one-year-old New Jersey bachelor who also happens to be founder and chief executive of the Boring Institute. The enterprise is dedicated to pinpointing, exposing and then harpooning the deadly features of modern life that Caruba says are turning us all into zombies.

Each year Caruba loads his elephant gun and goes hunting the

21

not-nearly-elusive-enough elements of tedium around us. In March, he announced his Most Boring Films of the Year Awards. In September, his institute gives the world its Fearless Forecasts of TV Flops and in December it's the grand finale — Most Boring Celebrities of the Year — Hollywood hams, Wall Street Wannabes and talk-show couch lizards who have received what Caruba calls "massive media overexposure."

Oh yes, and the Boring Institute has set aside an entire month for those dog days of summer when nothing happens and everyone's too hot to care. July is officially Anti-Boredom Month on the Boring Institute calender.

That's the thing about Caruba — he doesn't just whine and sneer about boredom, he frets about it, as well. Caruba is deeply concerned about its profound effects on young people, who, he says, are being warped by boredom.

Caruba spends all his spare time on the lookout for celebrities who have overstayed their welcome. Dr. Ruth Westheimer won the uncoveted Most Boring Celebrity Award a few years back. Last year the dishonour went to the ubiquitous Bill Cosby. As for the movies, Eddie Murphy's sewer-mouthed celluloid efforts won him the Boring Institute's Most Boring Film Award.

You don't have to be a tedious human to make it in Caruba's Hall of Infamy — he pillories inanimate objects, too. Self-help books are in there. So is any on-the-spot news hankie-twister about oil spills.

But there's one inanimate object that's conspicuously absent. It's a large, placid piece of real estate directly to the north of the Institute's New Jersey headquarters.

Canada. How come Canada isn't mentioned? Heck, the British and American press never tire of telling us how bland and unex-citing Canada is. Are we so boring that the Boring Institute hasn't noticed us? Nope. Caruba likes Canada. In fact he goes so far as to praise — hold on to your earmuffs, folks — Toronto. "An exciting city," he told me over the phone.

Oh dear. Caruba has a blind spot. It's a wonderful selfless thing that he's doing, but it's not worth squat if it lacks integrity.

I've got it. I know just what to send Alan Caruba to make him see the unexciting truth about Toronto: A pair of tickets to the next Leafs home game.

Gone Fishin' and Presumed Dead

I'VE GOT A LITTLE quiz for you. What would you say is the most dangerous Canadian recreational sport? I mean aside from such obviously suicidal pastimes as polar-bear wrestling, chain-saw juggling or trying to catch a flight out of Pearson International's Terminal One on a Sunday?

Motorcycle racing the most dangerous, would you think? Uh-uh.

Ice hockey? Downhill skiing? Nope and nope.

Karate? Scuba diving? Paddling down a river making noises like a mallard on the opening day of duck season? No, the sport that finishes more Canadians — more people in the province of Ontario, anyway — than all of the aforementioned is fishing. In the latest year for which the Ontario Medical Association has figures, twenty-one people went to the big fish camp in the sky, either from falling out of boats, or from having their boat sink, or from wading in over their heads, all while engaged in the deceptively gentle mania called angling.

Frankly, it doesn't surprise me. I've long thought fishing to be a treacherous and vicious undertaking that got much better press than it deserved. And if you think that sounds like sour grapes . . . you are absolutely right. If it was April, I would not be making these noises. April means spring, and spring means fishing fever.

Every spring I deck myself out in a goofy hat, rubber boots that go way higher than a decent rubber boot would go, and dig out my tackle box. I've got a tackle box plugged with lures and spinners and bobbers that would put Imelda Marcos's bedside vanity to shame. Each spring I lever it into the trunk of my car,

23

drive to some remote river bank in the pre-dawn gloom, pull on a silly vest with more pockets than a pike has teeth, assemble my ultralight Japanese-crafted graphite rod and wade into the water.

Usually about three hours of standing up to my pancreas in cold water does the trick. Usually after three hours, my eyes kind of focus, I shake my head and a tiny transcendent thought swims into my consciousness . . . What am I doing here?

That's when I remember that nothing ever happens when I fish, except I get cold and tired and kinda cranky. That's when I remember that I hate fishing. More than that — I hate fish. I don't like to eat 'em. I don't like to handle 'em. I don't even like to look at 'em. Fish (let's be honest here) are quite homely. You would never confuse a muskie or a hammerhead shark with Omar Sharif. Fish are ugly, they're slimy, they're smelly, they're fully of tiny sharp bones just itching to build a beaver dam against your tonsils . . . and they're so dumb that they don't even have the sense to come in out of the rain. But — and here's where true enlightenment comes in — but, I say to myself, if *they're* dumb, how come *you're* standing in a river trying to catch them? At least they're home! Which usually cures my fishing mania — for the season, at any rate. Next spring I'm gonna lick it permanently. I plan to spend opening day of the fishing season pursuing a safer, more sensible sport. Like maybe . . . skydiving with a wall safe strapped to my back.

Sealing the Fate of the Inuit

THERE'S A FAMOUS line from Browning that goes, "Oh, to be in England now that April's there . . ."

Well, we're still a few snowdrifts away from April and several thousand watery leagues from England, but you know if it were possible for you and me to stroll through the doors of London's Museum of Mankind this afternoon, we would find ourselves on the threshold of a very strange experience.

We would eventually fetch up against a combination kitchen-living room display that would look both alien and familiar. Certainly not English — there's a box of Pampers on the kitchen counter there, and a half-empty carton of Arctic Power detergent and some Carnation Instant Milk that make it feel pretty much like an average Canadian house.

But look at this in the corner — a huge box of raw, red, strong-smelling meat. And look there through the kitchen window — isn't that a . . . dogsled team?

Yes, indeed. The display is all part of an exhibit called *The Living Arctic: Hunters of the Canadian North*, showing in downtown London. The raw red meat in the box is seal . . . and there's a woman scraping a sealskin on the linoleum floor.

The purpose of the exhibit is to counter the powerful European anti-fur lobby by showing what Inuit life is really like and how important the seal hunt is. It's a real battle, because the anti-fur lobby has been very successful. With the help of photographic closeups of warm glistening eyes — both of seal pups and Brigitte Bardot — lobbyists have managed to persuade Europeans to boycott many Canadian products.

That's prompted Ottawa to make a series of appeasing gestures to Europe — many of them coffin nails for the traditional Inuit way of life. Recently we banned large-vessel offshore seal hunts. Good PR for us in Europe. Didn't cost you or me a cent.

But for many Inuit communities — suddenly no market to take their furs. Instant unemployment. Take Broughton Island, a tiny hamlet in Baffin Bay. There are — were — sixty Inuit teenagers on Broughton Island who are no longer being taught to hunt. Or much of anything else, I guess. In the past two years, twenty of those sixty have attempted suicide. Eight of them succeeded. Twenty out of sixty — 33 per cent of the teenage population. If it happened in a Toronto high school we'd call it an epidemic. Devote a full edition of "The Journal" to it. Appoint a Royal Commission.

We haven't done very well by the Inuit, you know. First we Christianized them by stripping them of their gods. Then we civilized them with whiskey and junk food and "I Love Lucy" reruns.

Now we tell them that their services are no longer required.

The numbers are fairly critical here. There are only 60,000 Inuit in the entire world — and only one-fifth of those in Canada. You know the town of Kapuskasing? Truro, Nova Scotia? Dawson Creek, B.C.? Any one of them has more citizens than the number of Inuit in Canada.

Don't get me wrong — I hold no brief for the fur industry and I don't hunt. But I also don't think I can stomach the prospect of protecting seals and placating Europeans by double-crossing the Inuit once again.

I guess what really galls is the thought of that Gallic Bimbo, Brigitte Bardot, emoting all over the TV cameras, saying, and I quote: "I beg you, I ask you from the bottom of my heart, I pray you with all the fervour in the world to prevent this hell from taking place on the Canadian ice banks."

Well, she saved some seals, I guess. But I'd have a lot more respect for Brigitte and the whole Animal Rights movement if they diverted one-tenth of the attention they lavish on cute and cuddly furry things and devoted it to Canada's original people.

But, as they say on Broughton Island, that will be the frosty Friday.

O Canada,
O Montreal

THERE'S A TENDENCY to think of Canada as the new kid on the block. Young . . . green . . . rawboned. But there's another Canada. You can get a taste of it standing on the north shore of the St. Lawrence just east of Lac St. Louis where it kind of bottle-necks in and the broad lazy flat St. Lawrence becomes a roiling maelstrom of white whipped froth and black swirling whirlpools. Jacques Cartier got this far, took one look and realized the doughty sea-weathered ships that had carried him across the Atlantic would be pounded to kindling in the Lachine Rapids. Cartier walked back to the Iroquois village of Hochelaga, clustered in the shadow of the extinct volcano that dominated the island and, thinking of the French king who was footing the bills and expecting him to sail straight to India, decided it might be politic to at least name something in honour of his royal backer. He dubbed the mountain "Mont Royal" . . . whence cometh "Montréal" or, for the cereal-box-reading impaired, Montreal.

Now that was in 1535. Michelangelo was coughing up marble dust in the Medici Palace in Florence. Shakespeare's father wasn't even a glint in Shakespeare's grandfather's eye. The American Revolution was still two and a half centuries to kickoff . . . and the spirit of Canada was flickering to life.

Montreal, at any rate — and for a good long time, Montreal *was* Canada. By 1750, more than a century before Confederation, 5,000 habitants called Montreal home. A hundred years after that it was the capital of our piece of North America. It's been invaded and occupied by French troops, British troops, American troops, whipped and shredded by riots and rebellions . . . it's been a

27

financial bastion . . . it's been a political powerhouse. Canada may be a rookie, but Montreal's a vet.

Of course, now there's the language thing — Bill 101 and all that. And true, in downtown Montreal, English signs are about as common as Edmonton Oiler sweaters. But it's more absurd than sinister. And even the Tongue Police are powerless in the face of serious twentieth-century commercialism. Hence, Le Dunkin Donuts.

And the fact is, a unilingual anglo is going to have a much easier time in Montreal, than a French-only Québécois is going to have in Calgary or Vancouver or Toronto.

I didn't speak any French on my visit to Montreal this time — partly because my French is fairly horrible, partly because I wanted to see what would happen. What happened was *pas de problème*. Taxi drivers, hotel clerks, shopkeepers, bartenders and folks on the street greeted me in French. When I responded in English, they smoothly double-clutched into Anglodrive with never a hint of a smirk or a sneer or even a Gallic shrug.

I had, in either official language, "a ball" in Montreal. Reggie Jackson once described himself as the straw that stirred the drink that was the New York Yankees. Well, for me Montreal is the vinaigrette, the dressing that flavours the enormous tossed and otherwise fairly bland salad that is Canada. Montreal is kind of elegant and saucy — like a Burmese with catnip. It provides something that we have to rifle the French language to find a word to describe — panache? Verve? Joie de vivre? Maybe it's Mount Royal itself. Maybe it's having an extinct volcano in its heart that makes Montreal Montreal.

Maybe poet Al Purdy said it best:

City of eye shadow and athletic priests
French poodles and exquisite buttocks
City of poets with enormous egos
And the wild high courting yard of the mountain.

Sam, You Wouldn't Recognize the Place

SOMETIMES I LIKE to fantasize about what certain famous, long-dead Canadians would make of our country today.

I imagine myself strolling along the banks of the St. Lawrence with Jean Talon or Alexander Mackenzie, Champlain or George Brown.

"What about scurvy?" Talon would ask me. "Is it still the scourge of the colony?" "No, no Jean," I would tell him. "We whipped scurvy long ago, thanks to Anita Bryant."

"And the trade route to the West?" Mackenzie would interrupt. "Is that still secure?" And I would explain to Alex in a soothing voice all about the Trans Canada, Air Canada and the strategic placement of Tim Horton Donut shops from sea to shining sea.

I would assure Champlain that the Iroquois (if not the Mohawks) were now safely and peacefully on board; I would convince George Brown that the Fenians were as scarce as Tories in a train station. I'd tell my ghostly friends that all the problems that plagued their lives had been efficiently settled.

At this point, I imagine Champlain becoming agitated and blustering. "Well, if you've taken care of all those problems, what in the *nom de Dieu* do you Canadiens worry about these days?"

And I put my arm around Champlain's shoulder and I say "Well, Sam . . . our big problem these days is . . . parking."

It is, you know. It is in my neck of the paved woods, anyhow. At Pearson International Airport there are parking meters that gouge you twenty-five cents for three minutes. You can pay up to twenty bucks a day for parking in parts of downtown Toronto —

if you can find a slot. Thanks to the political poleaxing of Via Rail, the cost of parking can only continue to spiral skyward while the phenomenon of vacant spots will rank right up there with unicorn and UFO sightings.

What's the answer — larger parking lots? We already have the largest parking lot in the world. The West Edmonton Mall boasts *covered* space for 20,000 vehicles. And, on the off chance extra company drops in, room outside for an overflow of 10,000 more.

Which depresses me. Parking lots are not the answer to the parking problem. They are only a quantum leap to a whole new level of parking problems, as in . . . now where the hell did I leave the car? Right now, on level three of the Terminal Two parking lot at Pearson, four automobiles of various hues and vintages sit corralled behind a mesh fence. They have flat tires, and their windshields are caked with months of dust and grime. They are orphan autos, separated from their owners returning from tropical getaways because said owners, doubtless befuddled with too many free Planters Punches, retained not the slightest clue where they had left their Oldsmobiles or Hondas. Surveying the multi-tiered maze of the parking garage, these owners wisely surmised that by the time they found their jalopies, the accumulated parking charges would exceed the value of the vehicles. And so the cars sit abandoned, a rusting parody of an elephant graveyard.

What can the rest of us — those still attached to our unparkable cars — do? Seek advice wherever we can, I guess. "I've solved my parking problem," says Henny Youngman. "I bought a parked car." Comedian Jim Samuels says, "I got no trouble parking. I drive a fork lift."

Funny. I tried those lines out on Champlain and George Brown and they looked at me oddly, as if I was coming down with a touch of cholera or something.

Words for Sale

A HH, LATE AUTUMN in Canada. The season when the leaves crisp and curl and tumble, the season when the air turns sharp and clear and the fields yield up their greens and golds in favour of sere ochres and sullen browns. A time for travel, too, the autumn. When woodland creatures grow butterball fat, then dozy, then turn and lumberingly look for winter dens and burrows. Every feathered critter with a brain cell in its tiny bird cranium tanks up and takes off for sunnier, more hospitable climes.

And one other rootless species takes flight — or foot — in the fall. The book-tour author. Every scribe or scribbler, hack or auteur who has in the previous twelve months managed to sandwich some pages of type between two covers goes on the great autumn book tour, crossing and recrossing this great land in seemingly meaningless routes. It's an annual migratory ritual. Look! There goes a crested Gzowski! And isn't that a golden Musgrave? And over there — oh, my! A white-tufted Robertson Davies in full fall plumage!

Actually most book tours are more about roosting than flying. You get to perch in a lot of bookstore windows behind stacks of your mint-fresh, patently *unsold* books and, wan smile pasted in place, meet people who loved your piece on . . . oh, they forget, but it was good. Or who think your documentary on taxi dispatchers was superb. Oh, that was Stuart McLean? Well, it was darn good, whoever did it.

Then there are the media interviews. If you are David Suzuki or Margaret Atwood, you get the big-name interviewers on the prime-time shows. If you are not David or Margaret, you get . . .

well, you might get the rock deejay desperately looking for something to fill the air vacuum between cuts from Def Leppard and the Clash. A surprisingly personable chappie, who chats warmly enough in the pre-inteview, suddenly claps on his earphones, thumbs his mike button on and barks something like "Okay, you're tuned to K-197 all-rock radio and we've got a major buzz for you right now . . . author Arthur Black right here in the K-197 booth. 'Zit goin', dude!!!!!"

The man sounds as if he's been sucking on a bag of helium. Incredibly, humiliatingly, you find yourself responding like some bad imitation of Donald Duck. "Well, thanks, Bob, and I gotta say it's great to be here . . ."

The questions you get on book tours are daunting, too. They range from "Where do you get your ideas, anyway?" (Well, there's an idea factory in Burbank, madam. You send them a blood sacrifice and thirty gallons of maple syrup and they send you three brainstorms a week . . .) to "What's Vicki Gabereau really like?" (Oh, she's a shy, retiring wisp of a thing, sir. She can only do her show with the help of massive doses of controlled substances.)

They look like fun, but they can be kind of gruelling, the autumn book tours. There's a lot of sipping of bad cups of machine coffee in airport lounges and railway depots. A lot of waking up in motels hard by the expressway, the headlights making tracer-bullet patterns on your wallpaper. There's a lot of sitting in bookstore windows, smiling, smiling, feeling your teeth go dry.

But there's a good side, too. You meet a lot of folks you otherwise wouldn't. You see a lot of places you otherwise might miss. And sometimes you just might get an idea for a commentary.

PART 2
Whom We Know

Yuppy Hobos

Now the joys of the road are chiefly these:
A crimson touch on the hard-wood trees;
A vagrant's morning wide and blue,
In early fall, when the wind walks, too;

BLISS CARMAN

A H, THE PLEASURES of the vagabond life! No nine-to-five scrabbling on the treadmill of wage slavery to make the car payments, the mortgage and a small dent in the orthodontist bills for your first-born's class-three malocclusions. No worries about crabgrass, a new boss or mustard stains on your Harry Rosen three-piece. Just . . . freedom. The freedom of the sun in your face and the wind at your throat. Vagabonds don't suffer from anxiety about whether the place they're going takes American Express, because (a) very few vagabonds carry American Express, and (b) empty boxcars and abandoned barns seldom take credit cards anyway.

We haven't heard much about the joys of being a penniless bum over the past few years. We've been too heavily into greed. People have been more interested in fleshing out their stock portfolios and sandblasting flophouses into trendy town houses.

But times change. I don't know if it was the stock market crash or if young folks have finally realized that twin BMWs, a vintage wine cellar and lifetime health club memberships do not a full life make, but interest in vagabondage is on the rise. I hold the proof in my hand. It's a new publication called *The Yuppy Hobo Travel Guide*.

It's no joke, either. *The Guide* is put out by — no guff, now — the National Hobo Association of Los Angeles, California. It includes an equipment and clothing checklist for the novice hobo;

a rundown of the ten fastest and the ten slowest freight trains in America; a chapter on hobo sign language, a glossary of hobo phrases (farmers are clover kickers, railroad police are cinder dicks) and even some favourite side-of-the-road hobo recipes such as *Coyote Slims Squirrel à l'Orange*, which starts with the juice of six stolen oranges and ends in a flambé of vodka or gin.

Curiosity got the best of me, so I tracked down the editor of *The Yuppy Hobo Travel Guide*. He turned out to be a young and yuppyish-looking Bobb Hopkins — actor by profession, "Santa Fe Bo" to his drifter friends when he leaves the glitzy world of L.A. and hits the open road.

He calls himself a "recreational hobo," which is to say that whenever the spirit moves him, Bobb Hopkins locks up his apartment, ties a few provisions into a bedroll and hops the nearest freight out of town. Sometimes it's just for a weekend; other times he stays out there until the snow flies. Santa Fe Bo says he's just the lead wave in a coming trend. He claims a "rebirth of the nomadic spirit" is under way. He admits the fact that you save a wad of money by hopping freights and sleeping under bridges doesn't hurt either.

But isn't it illegal and downright dangerous to hop freights? Yes and yes. Santa Fe Bo, with a nervous look over his shoulder at potential future lawsuits, hastens to explain that railroad bulls can indeed be mighty mean and he isn't advising anyone to actually get out there and throw his leg up on a moving boxcar.

But I don't think that Santa Fe Bo needs to worry. He knows that the chances of the average subscriber to *The Yuppy Hobo Travel Guide* actually riding the rails through the Rockies are about as good as the chances of the average purchaser of a Trans Am muscle car driving in the Grand Prix at Monaco. *The Yuppy Hobo Travel Guide* is about fantasies, not vacation plans.

Still, I can't help picturing some old bindlestiff picking his teeth and warming his hands over a can of sterno, as he watches some soft-handed, L. L. Bean-garbed would-be vagabond try to hop a freight. I can read the old-timer's thoughts from here. What, he is asking himself, the hell ever happened to good honest hobos?

Sign Here, Please

ONE MYSTERY I hope to unravel before I shuffle off to the big broadcast booth in the sky is the mystery of the autograph. Why do presumably sane human beings pursue, trade, track down, even pay for the signatures of other human beings? Oh, kids chasing down Lanny McDonald or Michael J. Fox I can understand — but grown people?

I mean, an autograph isn't good for anything. It's not as if you can eat them or get them changed into tens and twenties down at the bank or put them in your gas tank to improve your mileage. I suppose you could mount them and hang them on the wall of the den like trophy elk. Invite some friends over, give them a glass of port and a guided tour . . . "Yasssss, this is my Joe Clark. . . . And here's an early Maureen Forrester. Bagged that one outside the Royal York on a cold blustery evening just at dusk when the light was beginning to fade. . . ."

I dunno . . . sounds like a pretty boring party to me.

I'm obviously in a minority, though. A lot of people out there must love collecting autographs because it's big business. And I mean business. If you plan to snag the signatures of big-name baseball players, better bring your wallet along. Ball players used to give them away free; now they have rates. Pete Rose sells his scrawl for fifteen bucks. So does Jose Canseco. You can pick up a Roger Clemens autograph for nine dollars U.S., and for a ten-spot, Oriole pitcher Jim Palmer will sign his name on your undershorts.

Kind of a door crashers' special, I guess.

Don't expect the price of an autograph to go down just because the star in question has hung up his cleats either. Joe DiMaggio charges thirty dollars to put his name on your scrap of paper.

And I guess you can't really blame him. The players know that a lot of the autograph hounds are just going to turn around and sell the autographs to some other collector.

Now Picasso dealt with the autograph problem rather shrewdly. One day while he was relaxing on a French beach, a small child appeared with a piece of paper and a request for Picasso's signature. The painter knew the parents had sent the child and that their eyes were full of dollar signs, not admiration. So he turned the child around and drew a signed sketch on the kid's bare back. As the child scampered off, Picasso said, "I wonder if they'll ever let him wash?"

Ah, but I know of someone who handled the autograph problem even more graciously. He was a tall and venerable gentleman with silver flowing hair, famous around the world. One day on a train, two fidgety ladies approached him timidly and asked, "Have we the honour of speaking to the great Professor Albert Einstein?" He laughed and said they were mistaken, but he could understand it because he and the famous scientist did have similar hair. "Still," he said, "Dr. Einstein is a very old friend of mine. Would you like me to give you his autograph?"

And he did. The distinguished old gent signed a piece of paper that read "Albert Einstein, by way of his friend, Albert Schweitzer."

Take Your Breath Away

T HIS PIECE IS an abject apology to all the fans who were with
me — briefly — down at the local arena last Tuesday evening.

I understand why you abandoned me, left me to occupy the
entire east wall of bleachers by myself while all of you huddled
and crowded yourselves into the stands on the opposite side of
the ice.

I'm not upset with your decision to shun me. I don't blame you
a bit. No hard feelings.

It was the onions, wasn't it.

I knew it — knew it even when I was scarfing them down at
dinner before the hockey game. But I couldn't stop myself.

Usually, I am a man of reasonable self-control. You could walk
me through a boxcar full of cocaine and I wouldn't be tempted to
sniff. I don't do heroin or hashish, absinthe or anabolic steroids.
As for the number of times I've woken up in opium dens surrounded by geisha girls — I can count them on the fingers of one
mitten.

I am not a frequenter of booze cans, gambling dens or the
drawing rooms of houses of ill repute, but by cracky, show me a
chive or a shallot and my lower lip begins to tremble. Wave a leek
in my face and I whimper like a baby. Show me a Rubenesque
Spanish seductively shucking its onion skins in slow motion and
eee-yaw! — I turn into a ravening beast.

Yes, I'm an onion-luster. A harmless-enough mania, as addic-
tions go — aside from the friendship fallout. People just don't take
kindly to the thought of *tête-à-tête*-ing with someone whose
breath can set fire to eyelashes and melt mascara. That's why my

fellow hockey fans so enthusiastically vacated the entire east side of the arena last week. Considering the provocation (I'd eaten a fistful of green onions plus an order of garlic toast), I thought they handled themselves with poise and discretion, although I found the catcalls of "Beat it, flamethrower!" and "Hit the highway, laserbreath!" a tad overwrought. But I have to admit, if the tables were turned I'm not sure I'd want to get very chummy with a man who can singe cotton clothing and ignite paper articles by the simple act of exhalation.

Mind you, with a couple of Certs and a dollop of mouthwash I think I could mount a fairly spirited defence of the practice of onion eating. And I'd have plenty of evidence to back me up. Common sense, for starters. For centuries folk medicine practitioners around the world — from Confucius to my mother — have sworn by the efficacy of onions in warding off sniffles and sneezes. (Cynics don't dispute the cold-combating properties of onions; they say it's because no self-respecting virus could withstand the reek.)

And more good news — a study recently published in the *Journal of the National Cancer Institute* indicates that my favourite veggie can keep more than a bad case of sniffles at bay. The study, which was conducted by a joint team of U.S. and Chinese scientists, concluded that regular consumption of onions (and/or its elder cousin, garlic) significantly reduces the risk of stomach cancer. Previous studies have shown that onion eating lowers the risk of heart disease, but the cancer link is something new.

How does the lowly onion accomplish all this? No one knows for sure, but scientists think it may be the presence of allyl sulphide. That's a chemical found in all allium vegetables — which is to say garlic, chives, leeks, shallots, scallions and garden-variety onions. In laboratory experiments, allyl sulphide has been very effective in inhibiting the growth of cancer cells.

But I don't eat onions because I'm a health nut. To tell you the truth, I think I'd eat 'em if they were as hazardous to your health as smoking cigarettes or sitting through a Michael Wilson speech.

I eat onions for two reasons: first, they taste great; second, I like to think they keep vampires away.

Okay . . . three reasons.

They always get me the best seat at hockey games.

Also-rans of the World, Unite

VICTOR HUGO once wrote: "There is one thing stronger than all the armies of the world: and that is an idea whose time has come." I wish Victor had taken the trouble to pencil in the obvious corollary to that rule: "There is nothing more useless than an idea before its time." It's true. Alexander Graham Bell was laughed at for his idea that people could talk to one another over vast distances through a skinny wire. The public scorned J. A. D. McCurdy for thinking he could get an ungainly contraption called the Silver Dart off the ground. I'm sure if we could send Peter Mansbridge far enough back in time he'd bring us a report of riots and civil unrest in the Neanderthal valley cave complex where a mystic by the name of Urk had been stoned to death for fooling around with something he called "fire."

Don't even have to go that far back. Only a couple of hundred years ago we were burning so-called witches at the stake for thinking unfashionable thoughts.

Nowadays they'd probably have their own talk show.

Well, at the risk of courting a gravel shower or an in-depth hot foot, I'd like to put forth an idea whose time I think has come.

Mediocrity.

I believe the time has come to get down on our knees and venerate our second-bests, third-rates and also-rans.

That's what this country needs! Not a five-cent cigar or a chicken in every pot or toe rubbers that actually stay on or even a brain scan of Toronto Maple Leaf management — we need a coast-to-coast, tax-deductible, government-sponsored, non-denominational Church of Mediocrity!

Actually, it's not even an original idea. A Spanish writer by the name of José Ortega y Gasset suggested something like it years ago. He wrote: "What makes a nation great is not primarily its great men, but the stature of its innumerable mediocre ones." A few years ago, *New York Times* journalist Tom Wicker wrote an essay entitled "In Praise of Mediocrity" in which he suggested that America's quest for men of great intellect for the presidency was all wrong. Most Americans were mediocre, argued Wicker, therefore, did they not deserve mediocre leaders?

Unfortunately for Wicker, the next president of the United States was Gerald Ford, a man who put his thesis to the test and found it wanting.

As for Canada, well, we had our fling with the philosopher-king, Pierre Trudeau. Life did not noticeably improve under his reign.

As a matter of fact, we had never come closer to losing Quebec, the West and anyone in Washington who would accept a collect call than we did when the Lofty One patrolled the Bytown battlements. Canadians learned the lesson well — they went from voting in the Most Formidable Canadian in History to marking their ballots for Joe Who.

When you think about it, Canada could become a world leader — if that's not a contradiction in terms — in the worship of Mediocrity.

Heck, we've got the Toronto Maple Leafs, the Vancouver Canucks, the entire CFL, the city of Oshawa, a shadow cabinet minister whose actual name is . . . *Herb Gray!*

This country *knows* mediocre!

Besides, when it comes to mediocrity in human form, Canada can boast the . . . well, whatever the opposite of *crème de la crème* is. There is one Canadian who stands feet and ankles below the crowd when it comes to ordinariness. A paragon of pedestrianism, a chieftain of cheesiness, an absolute saint of the sub par and the so-so . . . a man who was mighty in name and nothing else . . .

William Lyon Mackenzie King.

This, ladies and gentlemen, was the world's Machiavelli of Mediocrity — a man whose best friend was his dog, who communed with shaving mirrors and predicted that Hitler would "rank someday with Joan of Arc."

This is the man whose most famous pronouncement was "conscription if necessary, but not necessarily conscription." Was ever a human immortalized for a more mediocre statement?

I think we ought to consider shifting our priorities. It's high time we gave up the Pursuit of Excellence and set our sights on the Achievement of Adequacy instead. I'm talking about a political action movement! A revolution, if necessary!

No, wait . . . that's radical rhetoric. Dangerous talk. We want something more, well, mediocre.

I know!

We'll appoint a Royal Commission!

And don't worry about that gentle humming sound.

That's just Mr. King purring in his grave.

Still Owl-like After All These Years

G OT A FUNNY sort of a time-warp treat when I turned on my TV the other evening. Instead of the usual peacock spray of colour blooming out of my screen, the picture came on in stark black and white. More than that. When the electrons finally settled, I saw, standing in the middle of a decidedly 1950s TV background, the owl-eyed, slab-sided terror of the TV courtroom, Perry Mason. Anybody out there too young to remember "Perry Mason"? Longest-running lawyer series in TV history. Perry Mason was dipsy-doodling around judges and turning hostile witnesses into lukewarm custard when Susan Dey of "L.A. Law" and even E. G. Marshall of "The Defenders" were too young to *reach* the bar, much less be called to it. The first Perry Mason show hit the airwaves in 1957 and the series stayed there till 1966. That was a long time ago. I'm pleased to report that not much has changed. Perry Mason still never smiles, never loses his temper. Paul Drake is still Paul Drake, with his silver pompadour and his loud sports jackets, still ever ready to run errands for Mr. M. "Paul, get over to city hall and find out how many males between the ages of twenty-six and thirty-nine applied for a fire permit last year."

Perry's righthand gofer, ever-present, ever-perky Della Street is still by his side. Good old dependable Della. Always alert, perenially permanented. Capable of taking care of anything from a sharp client to a dull pencil. Della and Paul were there on my TV, too, and so, on the far side of the courtroom, was the man who must hold the record as the losingest District Attorney in the history of jurisprudence, the inept but aptly named Hamilton Burger. Poor old Mr. Burger. Never won a case in nine full years. How'd he hold on to his job anyway?

At any rate it was, as I say, a treat to stumble across an episode of "Perry Mason" after all this time, even though the acting was a trifle more wooden and the plot a tad more contrived than I remembered.

How odd it was to run across a story in the newspaper the very next day — a story about Raymond Burr and his memories of portraying Perry Mason for all those years. His memories are not fond at all.

Burr talked of living in a cheaply furnished, Spartan bungalow right beside the Perry Mason set, of being summoned at three-thirty each morning to report for makeup, then working straight through until seven-thirty each night. He makes it sound as if the nine years of making "Perry Mason" were not much fun, and the ninth and final year was the least fun of all. Over lunch, Burr recalls, the producers assured him there would be a tenth and final season. He picked up his newspaper the next day to discover the series had been cancelled. "I wore a wristwatch that they'd bought for Mason to wear on the show five or six years before," recalls Burr. "I wore it on every show. I was in my dressing room no more than ten minutes after the last scene before they came over and asked for the watch. I gave them the watch and never saw any of them again."

Pretty shabby treatment for a fellow who made himself a household word around most of the planet. Still, I don't think Raymond Burr has too much to kick about. The series did make the ex-bit player from New Westminister, B.C., rich enough to buy his very own tropical island and several retreats around the globe.

And if by chance Mr. Burr is tuned in to the CBC right now at his Vancouver Island retreat, I have good news from an old fan, Raymond. After twenty-two years you still look exactly like . . . Perry Mason.

Remember Them

WELL, THIS YEAR it falls on a Saturday, I see. November 11. Remembrance Day. The day we're supposed to remember them.

Getting harder, of course, as the years go by. Anybody who was old enough to fight in World War I would be in his nineties now. Heck, it's been more than four decades since the end of World War II. All those young legs and strong backs who signed up to fight the second War to End All Wars now belong to men and women either well into the old-age pension or looking it smack in the face.

Me, I don't remember much first-hand — I was born in the middle of WW II. I remember radio ads for War Bonds and I think I can remember my mother grumbling about butter and meat rations, but that's about it.

Well, there is one more item . . . this token thing I have. You know those round souvenir discs you can buy at train stations and country fairs sometimes?

They look like a cheap aluminum sheriff's badge but you can punch out your own message on it. Pete loves Sandy. Rick and Lorraine forever — that sort of thing.

On the one I've got, the message reads: "HILDA. REMEMBER ME. BILLY CRERAR, AUGUST 27TH, 1941." Obviously Hilda didn't. Or maybe Hilda lost it, or died. I picked up the token for twenty-five cents in a flea market about ten years ago. I can't prove that Billy Crerar was a soldier and Hilda was his lover, but the date is right and I like to think so. Besides I couldn't resist that message — Remember Me. It reminded me of a Canadian wartime photograph I've never been able to get out of my head. It shows a long line of Canadian soldiers, Lee Enfields in hand, smiles on faces, marching up the main street of some anonymous Canadian city back in the early days of World War II. There's a shabby two-storey red-brick building in the background with "Premier Hotel" painted on the side of it. There's an old truck laden with hay bales parked in front of the hotel.

And breaking into the long khaki crocodile line of men — just streaking in from the left front edge of the photo — is a blond, five- or six-year-old boy running, hand outstretched, to clasp his soldier/father's hand one last time before — I guess — dad ships out overseas.

The father's cradling his rifle so he can reach a hand back for the boy. Remember me, both hands seem to say . . . remember me.

Remember me. Those were the last words of a Polish girl in the Ravensbruck concentration camp just before she was hanged by the Germans, back in '42. She was fourteen years old.

Remember Me. That's the title of a book by Edward Meade, who wrote about Canadian soldiers going and Canadian women and children staying during World War II. Here's an excerpt.

> *The troop train began to move. The soldier drew his wife to him again. Their kiss, ineffably soft and gentle, seemed to fuse them. Then he turned and sprang on the last car. The train was crowded with faces and he was one of them, but she could not see him. She stood for a long time on the platform, her eyes fixed on the trail of smoke against the sky. Gradually there stole over her the sensation that the flame of her life had left her, and she was only a shell. She felt cold and empty. When she got home, she sat for a long time listening to the silence of the room.*

It's getting tougher each year to remember them — the ones who stayed and the ones who went over and suffered as we who never had to go can't even imagine.

Tougher every year. But it would be obscene to forget them.

Shall We Dance

YOU KNOW WHAT I'd like to do to Darlene Scott? I'd like to give her a great big hug. I've never met Darlene, but I know I'd like her. Well, you would, too. Darlene's a good socializer. She's outgoing and spontaneous. She's demonstrative, not afraid to show her feelings. In fact, it's those very qualities that have put Darlene in dire need of a big hug. Her spontaneity got her in trouble with the law.

It happened like this: Darlene is a nurse's aide. She's thirty-one years old, a single parent with two young daughters. She lives and works in Palm Springs, Florida. One afternoon a while back, Darlene Scott came home from a hard day at work, kissed her kids, put a casserole in the oven and hopped into the shower to freshen up.

Oh, one other thing. She put the radio on so she could listen to some music while she was in the shower.

So Darlene's drying her hair, the kids are playing in the living room . . . and a Gladys Knight song comes on the radio. I can't prove it, but I like to think it was "Midnight Train to Georgia."

Well, if you're feeling good, and you're with folks you love and there's food in the fridge and the hassles of the day are behind you, you can't not dance when Gladys Knight sings "Midnight Train to Georgia." Which is what Darlene Scott did — she sashayed out of that shower and shimmied across the living room to the beat of the music from her radio. Her kids loved it. Darlene was having a ball. But some neighbours who'd been looking through the window were having a different reaction. They were calling the cops. The cops came and arrested Darlene Scott, took her to jail . . . and put the kids in separate foster homes.

Darlene Scott was charged with lewd and lascivious conduct in the presence of a child — the Peeping Toms claimed that she had been nude; Ms. Scott said she was wearing a bath towel.

The good news about this Kafkaesque nightmare is that it was a short one. Within two days the charges had been withdrawn and Darlene Scott was back home with her kids. But the good mood was gone. She didn't feel like dancing anymore. She is now suing the Palm Springs Public Safety Department for false arrest, harassment and false imprisonment.

I hope she wins. Even more, I hope she remains the kind of person who's not afraid to Pony or Hully Gully across the room when the rhythm strikes and the spirit takes her. I think she will. Dancers are an especially resilient breed. It's tough to keep 'em down. As another dancer, Freddie Austerlitz, proved. A few years back, Austerlitz danced his feet off in his first Hollywood screen test. The verdict from a talent scout was delivered in eight chilling words: "Can't act. Slightly bald. Can dance a little."

Sure could. Wasn't too long after that that Freddie Austerlitz changed his name to Fred Astaire.

Life in the Fast Lane

YOU KNOW HOW IT happens, eh? It sort of all unfolds like a bad dream, in slow motion. Except it's not, it's fast motion — that's the whole point. You're in your car going somewhere important and you're a few minutes late, as usual. You swoosh over the hill, notice out of the corner of your eye a car by the side of the road where there usually isn't a car. If the vision out of the corner of your eye is particularly acute, you may even notice a little black thingamajig mounted on the front window, driver's side, of the parked car. By this time your personal emergency headquarters in the back of your brain is feverishly punching out five-alarm phrases like unmarked car . . . radar . . . police . . . slow down . . . Maybe if your reaction time is very good, your right loafer has switched pedals and your car brakes are issuing a polite little eeeeeeeeeek. But it's too late. The officer is already climbing out of the unmarked car with his clipboard. In the next second or so he is going to wave you in for an unscheduled pit stop. You were speeding and you've been nailed.

I've never really figured out how to handle speeding tickets. I've tried everything short of slowing down. I've tried bluster. I've tried sulking. I've tried aw-shucks confessions of guilt and hey-pal-it's-a-jungle-out-there-but-we're-in-it-together. I've even tried flat-out, knees-on-the-pavement, tear-in-the-eye wheedling and begging, but I have never managed to talk my way out of a ticket. If I use my I-was-bad-but-I'll-be-good routine they just kind of nod and keep writing. If I try my who-do-you-think-you're-dealing-with number, they really go into high gear. "Well, sir, I was about to explain the offence you've been charged with, sir, but if you'd rather not hear it, sir, we could just meet again in court and discuss it in front of the judge, sir . . . and incidentally would you like to do up your seat belt and save yourself another $78.50, sir?"

Radar cops are the only people I know who can make *sir* sound like *lunkhead*.

Speeding tickets. It's very hard to wax philosophical about them. But if they do have a bright side, it's possible that PC Michael Ghrist is in charge of it. He's not in charge of anything else right now. Officer Ghrist has been suspended from the Louisville, Kentucky, police force. Why? For writing traffic tickets, that's why. Yep, police investigators discovered that in the past five years alone, Officer Ghrist has written out well over one thousand speeding tickets.

Which is not all that much for a full-time officer. But PC Ghrist's tickets are special. They're bogus. Each and every one of the tickets was issued to a driver who didn't exist.

"I just couldn't bring myself to write out real tickets," he told a police inquiry. "I had a heart. I started seeing the human beings behind the steering wheels."

And so Officer Ghrist just made 'em up! Still would be doing it if a whole bunch of "undeliverable" traffic violations hadn't turned up back at headquarters, raising some desk sergeant's suspicions.

I suspect the notoriety might prove too much for Officer Ghrist. Maybe he'll leave Louisville soon. Maybe he'll turn up behind a radar gun in your hometown. Or mine.

I already know what my new approach is going to be next time I get stopped.

I'm going to roll down my window, smile and say, "You wouldn't be Officer Ghrist, would you?"

Chess on
the Brain

I THINK IF I GET to come around in another lifetime, I would like to try to learn to play chess. I won't be mastering it this time around. I took a stab at it one rainy afternoon many years ago. The chess set was beautiful — all black and white marble. My teacher was patient and knowledgeable, my brain was still flexible and largely uncluttered. I memorized the various attributes of kings and queens and knights and pawns and then sat down to play my first game.

I lasted just long enough to get an unnerving glimpse of how mind-wrenchingly complex and convoluted the game is. I wanted to scream, Frisbee the chess board across the room and pound my knights and bishops and pawns into a rubble of undifferentiated marble dust. My mentor must have noticed the steam coming from my ears. He boxed the chess men and folded up the board.

"You," he murmured gently, "do not have quite the proper temperament to play chess."

Indeed. A little too much of Conan the Barbarian in my makeup, I'm afraid.

Not that the game of chess turns out noticeably noble champions. An American by the name of D. Keith Mano wrote: "Men who play at the grandmaster level are, almost without exception, strange and unpleasant."

Most experts say the best chess player who ever lived was a nineteenth-century lad from New Orleans named Paul Morphy. Morphy began his career as a gracious and soft-spoken member of the Southern gentry. He ended it a few years later, refusing to play or discuss chess, puttering about in a gloomy cave of a house obsessed with the idea that people were trying to poison him. He died of hypothermia in his own bathtub. He was forty-seven.

There have been weirder chess champions than Paul Morphy. Bobby Fischer, for instance. He was the American who electrified the planet by trouncing the Russian, Boris Spassky, for the world chess championship back in 1972. Fischer was a boy genius. He won the U.S. Championship when he was just fourteen. He was only twenty-nine when he thumped Spassky in Reykjavik, Iceland. Fischer showed the world that he was inventive, daring, adventurous and above all an absolute genius on the board.

But Bobby Fischer was not a nice man.

As a matter of fact, Mr. Fischer was a creep. He took obvious and sadistic pleasure in destroying his chess opponents, snickering, sneering and even applauding his own moves. "Chess is like war on a board," Fischer once said. "The object is to crush a man's mind."

Something's certainly applying undue pressure to Bobby Fischer's mind these days. He doesn't enter chess tournaments any more. He's refused to defend his title for the past dozen years.

These days, Fischer spends his time riding a transit bus back and forth between Pasadena and Los Angeles all day long. He memorizes books promoting anti-Semitism and white supremacy. You can buy a ticket on that transit bus, take a seat beside Mr. Fischer and blurt out "Protocols of the Learned Elders of Zion, page thirty-five, paragraph four." And Bobby Fischer will recite the exact words, complete with punctuation.

Then there's Viktor Korchnoi. He's a chess star, too. Unlike Paul Morphy, Korchnoi's still alive. Unlike the deranged Bobby Fischer, Korchnoi is still playing championship chess.

As a matter of fact, Korchnoi has announced that he is winning a game against a Hungarian grandmaster by the name of Geza Maroczy.

There's just one tiny catch.

Maroczy expired in 1951. Korchnoi claims he's playing chess with a dead man.

How do you do that? Through a spiritual medium, of course. "Our medium doesn't even play chess," says Korchnoi.

Yeah, well . . . if you're as good at playing cards as you are at playing chess, Viktor, I wish you'd check your hand.

I don't think you're playing with a full deck.

Who's the Guy in the Wig?

EVER WONDER WHAT it must be like to be really, *really* famous? Like setting up your pup tent in one of the outer circles of Hell, I would imagine. Picasso once said that the tragedy of being famous is that you have to devote so much time to being famous. Which makes me think of all those cameramen punched out by Frank Sinatra over the years. Of all the opening baseballs thrown out by all the Orson Welleses, of all those supermarket inaugurations presided over by aging ex-astronauts.

Some folks flee the attention — the Garbos and the Brandos — but that only cranks up the spotlight intensity; others rush to it like smitten June bugs. You can see them late at night, leering unnaturally and laughing too loudly as they jockey for couch space on Letterman, Leno and Arsenio.

Then there are the ones who can't seem to make up their minds about fame one way or another. Like the skinny kid in the Sycamore Plaza mall in Simi Valley, California, not long ago.

He was not the kind of customer who brings waves of peace and contentment to the soul of a mall security guard. For one thing, his moustache was crooked and he was wearing a bad wig. For another, he was hanging around the diamond-ring display in the Zales Jewelry store, a branch of which had already been knocked over by guys wearing disguises. Security guards materialized and directed a store employee to call the cops, then surrounded the suspect and asked him quietly to step outside. He offered no resistance. He wasn't a thief he told them, he was just shopping. So why the dumb wig, they asked him. Why the novelty store moustache? I have to, said the suspect. I'm Michael Jackson.

He was, too. That's what Michael Jackson has to do if he wants to spend an afternoon just booting around, hanging out, like normal folks. He has to dress up in a disguise to do what you and I do when we're bored.

But what a piece of work this Michael Jackson is. He spends half his time cutting records and doing tours and filming pop commercials that ensure hundreds of millions of people know him right down to his kiss curl — and he spends the rest of his time closeted in his hermitage compound telling the world to go away.

Know what Michael Jackson needs? He needs a friend like Texas Guinan. Texas was a famous actress cum flapper who acted as a speakeasy hostess in New York in the 1920s. One night, Texas and her nightclub were just flying nicely when the front door caved in and a wedge of boys in blue swarmed in. "Run!" yelled the doorman. "It's a raid!" One of the guests was Eddie, a person whose name would not look good on the police blotter or in the gossip sheets next day. Texas Guinan grabbed the famous patron by the arm, wheeled him into the nightclub kitchen, plopped a chef's hat on his head and a skillet in his hand and boomed, "Here ya go, honey . . . just keep frying eggs till the law leaves."

And he did. And the police never did book Eddie. Or Edward VIII as he would later be known.

Lesson there for Michael Jackson, though. It's all very well to be royalty but it doesn't hurt to keep a little talent. It's fine to be a king, but can you cook?

Arrest That Man!

THE NIAGARA RIVER IS 4,115 miles shorter than the Nile; 2,605 miles shorter than the Mackenzie. It's about the distance Terry Fox or Steve Fonyo or Vicki Keith would cover in a really good day. The Niagara River is a mere thirty-odd miles long, a gash across the spine of the Niagara Escarpment that carries the waters from Lake Erie down into Lake Ontario. It has a geological hiccup halfway down its length called Niagara Falls. For the past three centuries, that hiccup has mesmerized millions from every corner of the earth.

You would think that the majesty and magnificence of Niagara's thundering cataracts and roiling whirlpool rapids would be sufficient unto themselves. That viewers would be content to simply view, in awe. But there's something in the human spirit — some human spirits, anyway — that perpetually cries out, "Huh! That's not so big! I could top that! Easy!"

Thus, the stunters. The tightrope walkers and barrel riders and other assorted death dancers who have challenged the falls and the treacherous rapids below them.

They have walked across the gorge on slippery ropes and wire cables wearing peach baskets on their feet, pushing wheelbarrows, carrying cookstoves, washing machines and other people on their backs. They have gone over the falls in oaken casks and plastic pickle barrels, in metal spheres and rubber balls and fiberglass tubes. They've gone over in capsules that look as if they came from Apollo moon missions. In flimsy slapdash contraptions made of inner tubes and fishing twine.

And they've paid the price. Many were drowned or smashed or

suffocated. Others . . . well, Charlie Stephens was an Englishman who went over the Falls in 1920 strapped inside a heavy, iron-hooped well-nigh-indestructable oaken barrel. The falls picked up that barrel like a cigarette butt in a toilet bowl. All they ever found of Charlie was his left arm, still clutching a canvas strap.

Charlie had a kind of typical pedigree for Niagara daredevils. A loner. A drifter. He'd done a little stunt flying and parachute jumping.

Dave Munday's like that. He's a diesel mechanic, lives alone beside his machine shop about a half hour's drive from the falls. He's done some parachute jumping and stunt flying, too. And any time now — any minute now — perhaps as I write, Dave Munday may be bobbing along in a barrel, Ping-Ponging off rocks, tumbling through rapids, heading for the lip of the Horseshoe Falls. After that he will plummet 160 vertical feet into a plunge basin studded with bus-size boulders where several million tons of water will pound on him until . . . well, that's nature's choice. His barrel may be trapped down there for hours — even days. Or it may be flattened like a tin can under a truck tire. Or the barrel may bob free and float downstream to a waiting police boat where Dave will be arrested and charged. Dave Munday knows the routine. He's already been over the falls once, but he's got it into his head that some people think his barrel was too fancy. So this time he's going over in a . . . well, a piece of junk, really. I've seen photos of it. I wouldn't trust it in the shallow end of the swimming pool. Dave Munday thinks it'll earn him respect. But barrel riders don't get respect and they don't get rich and they don't get famous. What they mostly get is dead. I've never said this about any other man, but I hope Dave Munday gets arrested. Above the falls, preferably. Below the falls, if necessary. Just so he comes out of it in handcuffs, and not a body bag.

Leather Humour

SOMEBODY ONCE ASKED Groucho Marx how he knew what was really funny from what was not, and Groucho, with much cigar tapping and waggling of those caterpillar eyebrows, replied, "Well, an amateur thinks it's funny if you dress a man up as an old lady, put him in a wheelchair and give the wheelchair a push that sends it spinning down a slope towards a stone wall. An amateur thinks that's funny. But for a pro, it's got to be a *real* old lady."

Good old Groucho. He was funny even when he was addressing the serious business of being funny.

It's not so easy any more, separating what is funny from what is not. It wasn't so long ago that any yukmeister from the office wit to a nightclub comedian could ladle out gay jokes, Newfie jokes, dumb blonde jokes — you could choose from a whole arsenal of minority zingers, every one just about guaranteed to draw a laugh. But tell one of those jokes at a party these days and you're apt to be met with stony stares and a return three-word one-liner that goes: "That's not funny."

Which is true. Minority jokes aren't funny. The pearl in the oyster of a minority joke is a tiny (sometimes not so tiny) grit of cruelty. The unspoken assumption that drives the joke is that the audience can laugh because the audience is superior to the victim in the punchline, be it a lazy black, a drunken Indian, a wild-eyed Arab or a dopey dame.

Well, the minority joke is on the wane and no loss, but all the same I get a little nervous when we start to judge humour for political correctness. There is a danger that the pendulum could swing too far. Maybe it already has. I notice that Ikea Canada is taking flak for some of its advertising. And the flak is coming from . . . the Advertising World itself.

You know when your advertising upsets advertisers that some serious toe-mashing is going on.

Ikea is, of course, the company that puts out a whole range of housewares from cupboards to cutlery. Well, there's a new Ikea TV commercial that features two sinister Hell's Angels types, all decked out in leather and tattoos.

In the TV commercial they stand like barbarian bookends on either side of a diminutive, meek-looking Ikea spokesman who cheeps about the attractions of Ikea products. The bikers scowl as he carols on about more colour and more selection and more variety, but when he says "and more leather," they leap to attention. Ikea sells leather furniture, see. The idea of bikers shopping for leather furniture at Ikea is hugely incongruous, which equals funny, right?

Not according to an editorial in an advertising weekly called *Marketing*. "What possessed them to use real bikers?" it thunders. "The very idea of doing it is outrageous. The fact they implemented it is incredible. Ikea may be prepared to do business with bikers and accept them into the advertising and marketing fraternity. We do not."

So far nobody else has taken the Mrs. Grundian stance of the *Marketing* editorial writer. Ikea's advertising manager refuses to be spooked. "We like to have a sense of humour in our advertising," he says.

And the bikers? The advertising man says they seemed like nice guys to him. "When I got to the commercial shoot," he says, "they were already there, drinking Perrier water."

Perrier, huh? Some of us may have trouble seeing the humour in bikers, but it seems they have no trouble having a laugh on us.

What's a Clerihew, Anyhew?

I'VE BEEN THINKING about four men who gave their names to the world of humour. They are: Mr. Thomas Swift, the Reverend Spooner, Edmund Bentley and Claude Emile Jean-Baptiste Litre.

The first two are the best known. Mr. Swift gave us the famous "Tom Swiftie" jokes, as in: "Hmmm, sun's going down," said Tom darkly.

And "Am I ever getting fat," declared Tom roundly.

Also my favourite: "Why, that chicken has no beak," the man pronounced impeccably.

Those are all Tom Swifties.

He explained rapidly.

Spoonerisms, on the other hand, are rather more complicated. They owe their existence to the Reverend William Archibald Spooner, a turn-of-the-century Oxford dean who had the unfortunate habit of transposing letters in the words he spoke. Often very critical letters.

Thus, a toast from the lips of the Reverend to dear old Queen Victoria came out, "Let us drink to the queer old dean."

And who can forget the famous Spooner sermon that contained the phrase: "Ah, but our Lord is a shoving leopard."

Edmund Bentley was another old Englishman with an equally odd perspective on the English tongue. He liked to write little poems about famous people. People like Voltaire. Of him, Bentley wrote:

It was a weakness of Voltaire's
To forget to say his prayers

And which, to his shame
He never overcame.

What to call these fey little quatrains invented by Edmund Bentley? Edmunds? Bentleys? No. Edmund is too common and a Bentley is a car. Fortunately Edmund Bentley had a middle name that fits the bill perfectly. Which is why we call his comic inventions "clerihews."

And that brings us to the fourth man I mentioned: Claude Emile Jean-Baptiste Litre.

Monsieur Litre was an eighteenth-century maker of wine bottles and the father of the metric litre — facts that were largely lost in history until they were recently made public by researchers at the University of Waterloo, Ontario. Well, it's not often that major figures of science are forgotten, then rediscovered. The CBC carried the story. So did the *New York Times*. One Australian scientific journal called the Canadian discovery "a masterly account with an abundance of corroborative detail."

It may have been all that, but what it was not, was true. Claude Emile Jean-Baptiste Litre was a boozy April Fool's invention of a couple of folks in the science faculty at Waterloo, a revelation that was not received all that well by the boffins who'd been taken in by the joke. One British science anthology editor who'd swallowed the litre lampoon and written about it sniffed, "It is assumed that communications from established scientists are sincere."

Aw, lighten up, sir. Monsieur Litre should be taken in the same spirit as that poem about your countryman and colleague, Sir Humphry Davy, the famous British scientist. You know the poem?

Sir Humphry Davy
Abominated gravy
He lived in the odium
Of having discovered sodium.

That's a clerihew — from the master himself — Edmund Clerihew Bentley.

And that's that, Tom declared finally.

Go, Ashrita, Go!

H ERE ARE THREE things I am certain of:

    (1) I am typing these words.

    (2) You are reading these words.

    (3) Ashrita Furman is doing neither. He is joggling instead.

Yes, joggling. It's what Ashrita calls it when he laces on his running shoes, picks up three balls and goes out for a run. He juggles while he jogs — ergo, joggling. And we are not talking about twice-around-the-cinder-track fun runs here. Ashrita Furman runs — er, joggles — *full twenty-six-mile marathons.*

You'd never know it to look at the guy. Ashrita Furman is a smallish, trim thirty-six-year-old with short black hair, an easy smile and just a hint of a Big Apple bray in his voice. He manages a health food store in the Queens section of New York most days, but it's what he does when he leaves the store that makes jaws drop and brain pans strain at their moorings.

Here are just some of Ashrita's, umm, achievements:

Jumping Jacks. You know those dopey things that sadistic gym teacher made you do in high school — legs apart, arms outstretched, then legs together, arms over your head? The ones that made your legs twitch and your breath rattle in your throat? Furman did 'em for twelve straight hours. Twelve hours and twenty minutes, to be precise. Forty-five thousand and twenty-seven jumping jacks.

Skip Running. Another Furman refinement on the otherwise dreary pastime of running — running while skipping rope. Ashrita ran/skipped ten miles in a little over an hour.

Long-Distance Pogo-Sticking. Maybe by now you're getting

jaded with Ashrita's performances. Maybe you think the fact he went 11.6 miles on a pogo stick is no big deal. And maybe it wouldn't be — if he hadn't pogo-sticked the 11.6 miles up Mount Fuji.

Underwater Pogo-Sticking. Yes, he's done that, too. For five hours and thirty-eight minutes in San Francisco Bay. And more spectacularly, if not quite as long, in the piranha-infested waters of the Amazon River. (Only three hours and forty minutes there — the stick kept getting stuck in the clay river bottom.)

Milk-Bottle Balancing. Ashrita wondered how long he could balance a bottle of milk on his head without spilling it. So he got a bottle of two per cent out of the fridge, popped it on his noggin and went for a stroll. Twenty-four miles later, he stopped.

Long-Distance Stretcher-Bearing. Ashrita's only "tag team" event. He and three others carried a stretcher (with 140 pounds of weight on it) 127 miles in forty-four hours.

It would be difficult to choose Furman's most bizarre feat. He once clapped his hands in front of Lincoln Center in New York longer than anyone else ever has. Loudly and often — one clap every two seconds, audible from 100 yards. Try that one for a half hour. Ashrita did it for fifty hours and seventeen minutes.

He has also recreated Paul Revere's ride. Back in 1775, the Boston patriot made the original trip on horseback. Ashrita Furman *somersaulted* the whole thirteen and a quarter miles — 8,341 forward rolls by actual count.

Right now, Ashrita is warming up his pogo stick again. He's planning an assault on the Eiffel Tower in Paris. Wants to be the first person to pogo-stick up the steps right to the top. Which is not as easy as it sounds — what am I *saying?* — which is more difficult than some of Ashrita's other feats. Apparently the steps are very narrow and he'll have trouble maintaining his balance. Ashrita's not worried. He plans to lash himself to the pogo stick and use ski poles to keep himself upright.

Why does Ashrita Furman put his poor body through all these crazy trials? Because he likes being a world champion. A record holder. And he is. The *Guinness Book of World Records* recognizes Ashrita Furman as the very best human on the planet when it comes to performing all the aforementioned feats.

But don't take my word for it. Look it up on page 587. And 445. And 621. And 429. And . . .

Not Your Usual, Well-Groomed Job Applicant

YOU KNOW WHAT I hate most about working for a living? Getting it. Work, I mean — the job interview. I hate 'em. They make my knees wobble and my throat go dry. They turn me into a lickspittly forelock-tugging (if I had a forelock) toady. Every time I go for a job interview I hear some silly clown telling fatuous lies and outrageous distortions about me, my work background and my ambitions for the future. And, worst insult of all, the swine is using my voice.

Still, even my most horrible job interview went better than Dan Pollock's. I've had some pretty disastrous encounters with personnel managers, but I've never, ever showed up for my interview dripping wet, caked with mud and with seaweed hanging out of my cuffs. Dan Pollock did. In Vancouver not long ago. And he was half an hour late, to boot.

It had already been quite a day for Dan. Just an hour or so earlier he'd been briskly striding along the edge of English Bay when he saw a curious thing. An elderly lady, fully dressed, walking . . . into English Bay. Dan Pollock yelled to her, "Hey, lady, what are you doing?" No answer. She was past her hips and wading deeper. Dan Pollock looked around, yelled some more and then, aw geez, took off his suit coat, dropped it on the sand and waded into the frigid bay waters after her. He got close enough to ask her why she was doing what she was doing. The lady told Pollock that she was old and sick and didn't have a place to live and nobody cared anymore.

"Somebody cares," said Dan Pollock, as he felt cold mud oozing into his shoes and watched the water sog the crease out of his pants. "I care."

But they were both out their depth now. Pollock was treading water. He wasn't sure he could reach her in time. He swam back to the beach and hailed a passing jogger. The jogger ignored him.

So Pollock slooshed across the beach to a hotel where he convinced a waiter to call the police. By the time Pollock got back to the beach, a couple of police had already arrived and hauled the unconscious woman out of the water. Dripping and shivering, Dan Pollock went back to pick up his suit coat and his umbrella where he'd dropped them — and discovered that while he'd been out in the bay trying to save the suicidal woman, somebody had stolen his wallet. He lost sixty dollars and all his identification.

So that's the Dan Pollock who showed up for the job interview — sopping wet, mud up to his knees, flat broke, unable to produce so much as a driver's licence or a social insurance number — and half an hour late, of course.

To give him credit, Dan Pollock didn't cringe or snivel or make up lies or excuses. He just told the manager what had happened and said he'd like to go home, change and come back later, if that was all right.

It was. He did. And you know what? He was hired. "I got the job," says Dan cheerfully. "Maybe that's the payoff."

Dan's just a kid yet. Doesn't know that for people with an attitude like his, the world is full of payoffs.

Even Litter Has a Silver Lining

Pollution is nothing but the resources we are not harvesting. We allow them to disperse because we've been ignorant of their value.
BUCKMINSTER FULLER

I REALIZE THIS IS bound to sound a trifle trivial in a world beset with nuclear missiles, terrorist fanatics and an AIDS scare, but, boy, the way we litter ticks me off.

I live in the country, and most mornings I go for a walk along a country road. Most mornings I could easily fill a couple of Glad bags with the pop cans, beer bottles, cigarette packages and plastic excrement from McDonald's and Kentucky Fried Chicken that have been flung by unthinking jerks into the ditches overnight.

That's just the casual litter. Sometimes the louts and slobs who uglify our byways put their tiny minds to it and really do a job. There's a spot on my walk where a lovely stream burbles over limestone boulders and into a small gorge right beside the road.

I'm afraid you'll have to take my word for it, though. The gorge is plugged with rotting mattresses, rusting refrigerators and sundry other lumps of detritus abandoned by citizens who couldn't be bothered to drive to the dump.

What do they think about, these creeps and clods who wind down their windows and shovel out their pickups onto public land? Not much, I guess. I don't imagine they think any more than the kids I pass outside the high school, who shuffle along leaving a wake of candy wrappers and cigarette cellophane behind them.

Of course when you think about it, they don't have much in the way of role models, do they? What are the executives of steel and pulp-and-paper mills thinking about when they pump their crap into rivers, lakes and public air space? What are our farmers thinking about when they allow manure from their herds and chemicals from their fields to seep into streams?

What am I thinking about when I curse the cost of a catalytic converter on the exhaust system of my car?

We all "litter" in our own lazy ways, and sometimes it seems as if the whole thing is just too complex to be bothered with.

Don't, however, try to convince Dr. Wilbert Danner of that.

Dr. Danner is a professor of geology at the University of British Columbia. He, too, is addicted to morning walks. He, too, was distressed by the slough of trash he had to wade through to take them.

But then Dr. Danner had his moment of truth. He came to a discarded beer bottle, and instead of cursing it, he picked it up and put it in his knapsack. Same with the next one. And the next. Very soon the professor's knapsack was a-bulge to bursting, so the next day he took a bag with him. The bag became a fixture of his morning walks.

That was a few years ago. Dr. Danner is, if anything, an even more avid beer-and-pop-bottle-can collector nowadays. He's also made a few converts who scour the ditches and roadsides with him.

They make much? Thousands. Enough to create a university scholarship fund. The nickels and dimes the doctor and his cohorts receive for the returns they collect go into the Beer, Pop Bottle, Can Deposit Refund Bursary. Professor Danner and his scavengers find enough bottles and cans to swell the bursary by more than $1,000 each year.

I don't suppose many of us would be as dedicated or tenacious as Dr. Danner when it comes to scrounging, but I know one thing: if every Canadian picked up just one beer bottle today, the ditches of this nation would be some twenty-five million beer bottles lighter come nightfall. And at a nickel a bottle refund, there'd be some $1.25 million floating around between your pockets and mine.

Sounds like good business to me.

PART 3
The Things We Say

Whitewashing the Bard

FOLKS WHO WENT to the Shakespearean Festival in Stratford, Ontario, to see *The Merchant of Venice* saved a couple of bucks on the babysitter. They got be home early. The Stratford producers dropped a couple of scenes from the famous play. Matter of fact, they've lopped the entire rump of the play right off. You know, where Shylock, the Jewish villain, is forced to convert to Christianity? That's gone. "In Shakespeare's time people believed the conversion was merciful," said a production spokesman, "but today such a belief is abhorrent, meaningless and insulting."

Well, exactly. It's about time somebody exposed that seedy old bigot Shakespeare — and I trust they won't restrict their timely sanitizing service to the one play. Let's face it — the Overblown Bard of Avon is overdue for a major overhaul. Let's hope that in the future we can look forward to news stories such as:

STRATFORD, MAY 1993. Festival organizers have announced that this year's production of the Shakespearean tragedy *Romeo and Juliet* has been revised, following criticisms that the ancient play was sexist and ageist. "We acknowledge that the original characters were woefully underage," said a Stratford spokesperson, "and that their paranoid heterosexuality indirectly slanders other forms of valid interpersonal relationship."

In the updated production, retitled *Romeo and Jules*, two mature students explore the pitfalls of maintaining a meaningful gay relationship in post-Renaissance Italy.

STRATFORD, MAY 1994. Organizers of the Stratford Shakespearean Festival announced that this year's production of *King Lear* will be subjected to an extensive reworking. "Viewed through twentieth-century eyes," said a festival spokesperson, "the original script is really quite unacceptable. Not only does the play ridicule mental illness and ageing, the very title glorifies monarchy, and the hero's name itself carries offensive overtones. King 'Lear' . . . really."

In the revised work, the hero, Citizen Peekaboo, strolls the heath wearing waterwings and flip-flops while delivering a comic monologue about learning to live with middle-age spread and a receding hairline.

STRATFORD, MAY 1995. There will be only minor changes in the offerings at Stratford's Shakespearean Festival this season. "We recognize that there have been some major revisions in our presentations over the past few seasons," says a festival spokesperson. "This year, we're restricting ourselves to one or two small cosmetic touchups."

The spokesperson noted that in deference to Animal Rights activists, *The Taming of the Shrew* has been retitled *Mole Rats Are People, Too!* She also noted that for similar reasons one small scene has been dropped from the production of *Macbeth*. "We feared that when Lady Macbeth scrubs her hand and screams 'Out damned spot,' some people might think she was verbally abusing her Dalmatian."

STRATFORD, MAY 1999. The Bard has been kicked out of Stratford. For the first time since its inception in 1953, the Stratford Shakespearean Festival will not feature any Shakespeare plays. "His plays have simply become too controversial," a festival spokesperson explained. "This year we're going to a musical format. Anne Murray singing the complete works of Winnie the Pooh as scored by Dan Hill. If this brings the audiences back, and we think it will, then All's Well That Ends Well."

Simple English Will Suffice

S OMETIMES I GET the feeling I'm coming down with some kind of linguistic Alzheimer's disease. I don't seem to comprehend the English language any more — large chunks of it, anyway. Consider: here I am sitting in a Dunkin Donuts coffee shop, contemplating a tiny, fluted plastic tub with a tinfoil top that tells me it is "non-aerated dairy creamer."

What the hell is that?

I've got a letter from Revenue Canada in my pocket that contains this paragraph: "Subtract Total Personal Exemptions on line 45 from Net Income on line 41 and enter the result on line 46. Subtract line 59 from line 46 and you will have arrived at your Taxable Income on line 60. Carry it to page four."

Jargobabble — it's everywhere. Military types drone sonorously about anti-personnel devices; they mean lethal weapons. Smiling Al down at the car lot tries to sell me a "pre-owned" (used) Oldsmobile with brand-new "impact attenuators" (bumpers).

You think it's better in the Groves of Academe? Here's a fragment of a letter from an academic: "The colleges, trying to remediate increasing numbers of . . . illiterates up to college levels, are being highschoolized."

Read it and weep — the writer is a professor of graduate English at an American university.

When it comes to larding up the language, academics do it, soldiers do it, governments and ad writers and God knows journalists do it. But no slice of the human pie jargonizes and fuzzifies quite as thoroughly and enthusiastically as the business sector.

Business English — a whole horror story in its own write.

Business scribes are the people who gave us such excrescences as "prioritize" and "containerization." They're the folks who can twist a simple phrase such as "about your last letter" into something like "re yours of the fifth inst."

Well, I'm delighted to report that there's a wee glint of sunshine on the "bizlit" horizon — two glimmers, actually. One is the birth of the Percy. The Percy takes its name from that deadly phrase with which many an equally mordant memo begins — "pursuant to your request . . ." A Percy is an award, like a Grammy, an Emmy or an Oscar. All you have to do to win a Percy is pen the worst memo or business letter in any given year.

Percys are awarded in several categories, including "Make My Day" for the memo or letter with the most anger seeping through; "Mrs. Malaprop," for the submission with the most misused words and phrases; and "Stuffed Shirt," which is awarded for the business missive using the most jargon and antiquated phraseology.

If you've got a contender in your In basket, send it to The Communications Workshop, 217 East Eighty-fifth Street, Suite 442, New York, N.Y. 10028.

More good news for business English comes from Britain, where the U.K. Civil Service, 500,000 paperpushers strong, has just received a pamphlet enjoining them to speak and write clearly and concisely.

The pamphlet calls on champions ranging from ex-prime minister Thatcher ("It is no exaggeration to describe plain English as a fundamental tool of good government") to the Bible: "Let thy speech be short, comprehending much in few words." Ecclesiastics 32:8.

I'm sure the campaign will be a huge success. The Brits have a talent for this sort of thing when they put their mind to it.

As was demonstrated by the British military commander Sir Charles Napier, who in the nineteenth century besieged and conquered the Indian province of Sind.

His one-word communiqué back to London headquarters: "Peccavi."

It's Latin for "I have sinned."

If Latin Is Dead, Why Won't It Lie Down?

Y OU CAN CONSIDER this piece an, umm, apologia, I suppose. That's because a few weeks ago I was nattering away about something or other and mentioned in passing that Latin was "after all, a dead language."

The obituary was premature.

Since then I have learned about the work of Abbot Carlo Egger and Lamberto Pigini. Abbot Egger lives and works in the Vatican, while Signor Pigini toils in a tiny office in the Adriatic city of Recanati, but they share a common goal: to keep the classical language of Latin alive and breathing.

Even more than that — they're doing their level best to Latinize the twentieth century.

Abbot Egger heads up the Vatican's Latinitas Foundation. One of the chores he performs in that capacity is to read the newspapers and render current events into the language of Cicero.

I mean, *really* current events. Remember the war in the Falklands? When Abbot Egger writes about that, it's *Bellum in Insulis Falclandicis.* You thought Ben Johnson got tripped up by steroids? Nope, it was *usus agonisticus medicamenti stupefactivi.*

Abbot Egger can get downright contemporary when he works at it. He's figured out what Nero would have done if he'd wanted to wager a few sesterces on his favourite horse in the third race at the Coliseum racetrack. He'd have summoned his *relator pignore certantium.*

That's Latin for "bookie."

It's fascinating to speculate on just what Nero or any other ancient Roman would make of Abbot Egger's news roundups. What would they think of the twentieth-century fashion craze for *bracae lintaeae caeruleae*, which is to say "blue jeans"? How could they possibly comprehend *autocinetum pyrobolo dolose instructum*, "car bomb"? And you can only wonder how they would ever get a handle on *capacissima aeronavis Coreae Meridianae missilibus percussa ac praeceps deiecta*, which is what Abbot Egger types into his word processor when he's describing the Soviet downing of that South Korean airliner.

At least that's what he types when his word processor hasn't been neutered by a *fluoris electrici abruptio*, "a power blackout."

But it doesn't really matter how Ancient Romans would react to the abbot's work because he's not doing it for them. He's doing it for us. Abbot Egger is trying to convince you and me that not only is Latin not dead, it's alive and more than capable of handling anything the twentieth century can throw at it.

That's why he's publishing the first volume of his Italian-Latin lexicon next month. "It is proof," says Abbot Egger, "that Latin can be used even today to discuss everything."

Lamberto Pigini agrees. He's hard at work describing twentieth-century experience in Latin terms as well, though in a slightly different context.

Signor Pigini has already turned out several tomes. Let's see now, there's *Snupius*, and *Carolus Brunus* and of course *Michael Musculus*.

Or as we know them, Snoopy, Charlie Brown and Mickey Mouse.

Lamberto Pigini publishes comic strips in Latin. "We do this to make the language loved," says Pigini simply.

Well, some folks love Latin, I guess, though I've met a lot more who loath it, particularly high school students of the "*sum, esse,* phooey" stage of mastering the tongue. But love it or hate it, the one thing you can't do with Latin is ignore it. It's everywhere.

Suppose you journeyed by bus from Regina to Philadelphia via London, to enjoy a duo of minor celebrities with major egos debating the pros and cons of civic propaganda versus media innuendo in an arena, stadium or auditorium at 7:00 a.m. on a Saturday in August.

There are forty-seven words in that sentence. Twenty-one of them are pure Latin; almost all the others come from Latin roots.

Latin dead? That's some display of (ahem) rigor mortis.

There Should Be a Word for It

BACK IN THE LAST CENTURY an Englishman by the name of Sir John Lubbock looked at and listened to the babble surrounding him and wrote, "The English tongue is rapidly spreading and bids fair to become the general language of the human race." So far, Sir John was wrong, but he was close. Of the nine thousand-odd languages and dialects parcelled out among the five billion-odd language speakers on this earth, English is the second most popular, after Mandarin. Sometimes it's hard to figure why. Any language that would allow four letters — *o-u-g-h* — to be pronounced *uff, oo, owe, off, up* and *ow* — as in rough, through, thorough, cough, hiccough and plough — would not, you'd think, be an immediate front runner in the semantic sweepstakes. Still, English is convenient in its own way. It has an arsenal of 800,000 words, but you need master a mere 2,000 to take care of 99 per cent of all conversation. In fact if you can get your tongue around just eleven words — I, the, of, and, a, to, in, that, is, it and you — you'll be covered for fully 25 per cent of all words spoken in a typical English conversation.

Maybe that accounts for its popularity. Because it is popular, right around the world. English is staging a bloodless coup just about everywhere you go these days. German workers grumble about working under *der Boss.* Young energetic Italians are signing up for *il body building,* adventurous French are going in for *le rafting* and *le trekking.* And in Japan . . . well, as the number-one hit pop song of a couple of years ago put it: *let's dancin' people . . . hoshi kuzu nagarete feelin' so good.* I'm probably a little shaky on the tune, but those are the actual lyrics.

But even with 800,000 words to draw on, English sometimes falls short of being perfect. Often it lacks — well, what the French call *le mot juste* — the perfect word or phrase for a phenomenon or a situation.

I figure we've lent enough words to other languages, why not borrow some back? Herewith a few foreign words that I think would nicely flesh out the English portfolio:

First, *far potch ket.* You know when you're moving the lawnmower in the garage and you notice there's a tiny screw loose in the carburetor, so you bend over to tighten it, but it's connected to a smaller butterfly-shaped doodad that seems to be out of place so you twiddle that around, too, only that loosens the bell housing and the gasket slips right out and gasoline spurts on to the sleeve of your good shirt and the gasket falls on the floor and you can't remember if it's white side out or the other way around? That's what Yiddish calls *far potch ket* — all fouled up, especially as a result of your trying to fix it.

Here's a poignant offering from Russian: *ros-blee-OO-toe.* That's a phrase you use for someone you once loved. (Ah, my sweet *ros-blee-OO-toe* . . . she was mah lahf. . . .")

What do you call that dreadful bore who corners you at cocktail parties . . . buttonholes you? Won't let you go? If you're Italian, you call him an *at-tahka-bo-tone-ee.* We could use that word.

We could use *Fire-ah-bend*, a German word for that giddy party mood you feel at the end of a working day. We could use *Katzenjammer*, another German word for a killer hangover. We could use the Bantu phrase *Em-boo-kee em-voo-kee.* Which is what Bantus say when they feel like shucking off their clothes and dancing.

Aw, what the heck, I know its still early, but I'm in a *fire-ah-bend-ish* kinda mood. I don't care about tomorrow's *Katzenjammer* — let's *embookee emvookee.* I'll put on that hit record: *"Let's dancin' people . . . hoshi kuzu nagarete feelin' so good."*

Yeah, yeah, yeah.

Eco-chic

WELL, WE'VE STILL got a long way to go before we can officially sweep the twentieth century into the sanitary-landfill site of history, but I've already got my nomination for most meaningless word of the century.

It's "environment."

Sturdy enough word, one would have thought. Served the French well for several hundred years as a *mot juste* meaning "around," "surrounding." We swiped it from them fair and square a couple of hundred years ago and have been using it ever since. Any decent language needs a robust four-legged Percheron of a word like "environment" to describe . . . well, everything that's *around*. It's absolutely essential. You wouldn't think a word like "environment" could be easily usurped, bled white and left by the road to die.

But I think we've lost it. Used it up. I knew the word was mortally wounded when I heard a television commercial burbling the virtues of a product that *cleans environmental surfaces!*

Turned out they were talking about a toilet-bowl cleanser. Then there was the story about a new municipal labour group receiving formal approval from the City of London. The group calls itself the Worshipful Company of Environmental Cleaners. What's that, you ask? Well, that's an organization made up of what had been called Municipal Cleansing Operatives. Come again, you persist? Well, you probably remember when we called them road sweepers and garbage men.

That was the beginning of the end for the word "environment." The death knell sounded when the politicians hell-bent for election in both Ottawa and Washington picked up the Envirofootball and began to scuttle downfield.

Being pro-environment is suddenly terribly chic. And why not? It's a terrifically safe platform. Better even than opposing illiteracy, safer than calling for Senate reform. Who, after all, thinks we need more stinking rivers, dying trees and poisonous air? Besides, the environment isn't uppity like native people and senators. It just kind of lies there, taking a long time to get noticeably worse. Or better.

Given enough time, the politicians and their speech writers probably could have wrestled the word "environment" right to the mat, leaving it a meaningless gaggle of consonants — if it hadn't been for one thing. A news story out of the University of Chicago, where researchers have discovered that the latest victims of environmental degradation are . . . condoms. Safes aren't safe — they're susceptible to air pollution. The researchers exposed twenty condoms to air that was comparable to what you'd find in Los Angeles on a smoggy day. Result? Eighteen of them — 90 per cent — ended up looking like morning-after shots of the Hindenburg. The scientists' advice: your condoms should work fine as long as you keep them away from "heat, light and ozone."

Heat, light and air — or, put another way — the environment.

We were willing to put up with losing our lakes and rivers, maple syrup and rain forests . . . but condoms? That's hitting a little close to home. I tell ya, if scientists can ever prove that air pollution ruins the finish on our cars, we'll have this shabby old planet back in Garden of Eden shape before you can say "cleans environmental surfaces."

Reports from the Dairy Front — er, Rear

W E HUMANS HAVE hung some pretty strange handles on things in this world, but one of the strangest and most inappropriate names we ever came up with was the name Bossy for cows.

Bossy? Bossy means . . . commanding, domineering, overbearing. You ever meet a cow like that? Naw, cows are not bossy. Most of the cows I ever met (except for the odd stroppy one) were docile, passive, accepting. They just kinda hang out in the pasture there, staring off into space, those big jaws chewing mindlessly, kind of like Kelly Gruber with an udder. Cows are never paranoid, like a penful of porkers, or hysterical like a henhouse of White Leghorns. Cows are just *there* . . . to give. And holy cow, do they give. They give us milk, and cream and cheese and butter and antibiotics and when you get right down to it, Baskin-Robbins Swiss almond mocha double-dip cones. And, sad to say, when you get right *right* down to it, they also give us car seat covers, billfolds, belts, boots and the all-beef patty that goes in the sesame-seed bun.

You would think, given that we vacuum up just about everything the cow has to offer from the horns on her head to the glue in her hooves, you would think that at minimum we would, if not venerate the poor beast, at least speak well of her. But no, we're beginning to badmouth her, as well! Some environmentalists are fingering the cow as a major polluter of our rivers and lakes. They say that herds of cows are grazing the South American rain forests to oblivion, that cow meat is clogging our arteries and killing us off and — unkindest cut of all — that the cow is a major contributor to the global warming trend . . . because of uncontrolled cow flatulence.

Yes. The latest bovine slander has it that the cows that are chewing down all those rain forests to make all those artery-clogging burgers are giving themselves gas in the process. Methane gas. Cowherds of the world emit it by the megaton, and these dense clouds of cow-generated methane gas float skyward to join the other greenhouse gases befogging the planet.

Well, excuse me, but I doubt very much that any Holstein, Friesian, Ayrshire or Guernsey ever voted in favour of browsing through the Brazilian underbrush dodging piranha and jaguars all for the eventual privilege of sending cholesterol-laden burger bits into my left ventricle. You know those flashy neon statistics — over X billion burgers sold — that wasn't a cow's idea, you know. Call it a hunch, but I'm practically certain that the cows of the world would be overjoyed if we pulled them off the menus, out of the rain forests, away from the overcrowded feedlots and back into those nice green open pastures where they used to be. All we have to do to cut down on all the nasty side effects we're blaming cows for is stop breeding so many cows.

In the meantime, and until we smarten up, I trust the cows of the world will continue to chew their cud, get gas and . . . flatulate.

Considering how we treat them, I think it's particularly apt.

A Library Is a Library Is a Library

EVER THINK OF changing your name? I think about it some-times . . . but then I got sort of a funny one. Art Black. Arthur Black. Well, not as funny as Montmorency von Peppercorn, per-haps, but I do get the odd look, and that's okay. I mean, if it ever started to get to me, all I'd do is drop by my favourite bookstore in downtown Toronto just to listen to the clerks answer the phone. The store is called This Ain't the Rosedale Library. Yeah, that's the actual name over the door. This Ain't the Rosedale Library. No doubt the punchline of some long-gone inside joke. Thing is, that's what the people who work in the bookstore have to say everytime they answer the phone.

Which leads to conversations like this:

Brrrrrrinnnnnnnng

"This Ain't the Rosedale Library." (Pause)

"Beg pardon?" (Pause)

"No, ma'am, you've got a bookstore. This is the This Ain't the Rosedale Library bookstore." (Pause)

"No, ma'am, I wasn't being sarcastic. I know you know this ain't the Rosedale library, but that's the name of the bookstore. This is the This Ain't the Rosedale Library bookstore."

And so it goes at the This Ain't. Not only good books, but a great floor show.

Funny how some folks voluntarily take on names you know are going to torment them through life. Frank Zappa names his kids Dweezil and Moon Unit. Some Taffy prankster names a Welsh whistlestop Lanfairpwilgwin-gilgoggery-chwrindrobwillanty silliogo-gogoch.

Also known as St. Mary's church by the pool of the white hazel trees, near the rapid whirlpool, by the red cave of the church of St. Tysilio.

There's a lake in Massachussetts just slightly longer than its Indian name which is Charguggagog manchaugaggog chaubunag gungamaug.

Which, translated, means Lake you fish on your side, I'll fish on mine, no one fishes in the middle.

The settlement to the France versus Newfoundland Cod War should be so succinct.

Names don't have to be long to be perfect. Take Dorothy Parker's canary. She called him Onan. Because, she explained, he spilled his seed on the ground. Then there was the fellow who said that the only proper name for a pet aardvark was Emilion.

As in "Aardvark emillion miles for one of your smiles, my maaaaaaaaaaaaaaaaaaaamy."

Jean Cocteau once told Marlene Dietrich that she had a name that began like a caress and ended like the crack of a whip. That's not bad . . . but I don't think *my* mammy could ever bring herself to phone the office and ask for Marlene. Besides, I haven't got the legs.

Maybe I'll just become a Marxist. Groucho, not Karl. Groucho Black . . . whaddaya think?

Feels good and it's got a built-in escape hatch. As the original holder once said, waggling woolly eyebrows and tapping his pepperoni-length cigar: "Groucho is not my real name. I'm just breaking it in for a friend."

Just Tell Us What You Do

FOR NEARLY TWO YEARS I've been driving past a strange building on the way to work, trying to figure out what it is. It's one of those modern red-brick, bunker-style monstrosities, big as a Mulroney promise and radiating all the charm of a refrigerator carton. I figured once they'd bulldozed out the foundation and put in the structural steel, a big sign would go up saying what the building was for. Nope. The day I saw the roof going on, I said to myself, "Aha. Now we'll find out who the tenants of the building are." Wrong again. It wasn't until the sod was laid and workmen were painting stripes on the brand-new parking lot that a plastic sign went up on the lawn. It reads "Syntex." Swell. I'm no wiser than I was when the site belonged to woodchucks and dandelions.

I have no idea what Syntex is or does or makes, and the name is altogether too boring for me to bother finding out. Remember when business names actually *told* you what the business was about? General Motors made cars, Canadian National Railways ran trains and Massey Ferguson Farm Machinery was where you went to buy a tractor. Even brands that were a little vague could be deciphered. Esso for instance. Esso comes from the letters S.O., which stood for Standard Oil — a name that let you know they were in the Black Goo business.

Nowadays the marketplace is fogged in with blurry, androgynous company names like Biodyne, Alphatronix, Duosys and, well, Syntex. Can't tell if they're a business concern or a Liverpool punk fusion band.

Personally, I think computers are to blame. Most PCs limit the number of letters you can use to "name" a new file — eight letters

82

is about the maximum. This makes it tough for somebody who needs to create a file on, say, Agostino's Consolidated Tool and Die Incorporated. Which in turn explains how we end up with unfathomable and unpronounceable abominations like Agcotadi.

But there's some decidedly good news on the fuzzification front: the public isn't taking to the new computer-spawned brand names.

As a matter of fact, they hate 'em.

A San Francisco graphics consulting firm decided to take a survey last year and find out just what folks liked — and didn't like — in the way of brand names. The company dispatched interviewers with clipboards to shopping malls all across the continent. The clipboards contained 672 corporate brand names. More than a thousand people were buttonholed and cajoled into rating the brand names in terms of recognition and "likeability."

Surprise, surprise, the surveyors discovered that companies with names like Ford Motor, US Air and Remington Firearms — names that tell you what the companies do — scored very high with the people surveyed.

And what was at the bottom of the list? Dopey names. Meaningless, vague and unintelligible names. Names like Navistar, Primerica, Nynex and worst of all — Allegis. Those names don't reveal anything about the companies or their products. Two years ago US Steel decided to change its nice, simple, straightforward name to the incomprehensible USX Corp. Survey result? People ranked the former name in the top 50 per cent, the new name in the bottom 5 per cent.

You wouldn't think businessmen would need to be told that consumers prefer clarity to obscurity in a brand name, but apparently they do. The chief executive of Landor & Associates, the company that conducted the brand-name survey, shakes his head and says, "You have to wonder whether it's management's ego or naïveté or both. Why not link your name to your heritage, or a meaningful association, rather than picking those nonsensical names?"

Of course, the chief executive of Landor & Associates might know a bit more about that than most folks. His name is John Diefenbach — a name pretty close to one which, if memory serves, has a fair pinch of heritage and meaningful association on this side of the border.

Didn't This Used to Be Muddy York?

I DON'T KNOW HOW the past couple of years have been for you, but they've been very fulfilling for me. Take my command of Russian. I've increased it by a full 33 per cent. I used to know three Russian words: *da, nyet* and *sputnik*. Now I know four: *da, nyet, sputnik* and *glasnost*.

Ah yes, *glasnost*. Recent news from the Soviet Union indicates that whatever else *glasnost* may be, it is not retroactive. Not in the case of Leonid Brezhnev.

You remember Leonid — late Soviet strongman and leader of the Communist Party. On his death a few years ago, party hacks scrambled all over looking for things they could rename in Brezhnev's honour. They came up with a city, an atomic ice-breaker, a passenger liner, an army tank division, a metallurgical institute, a military academy, a nuclear reactor, a dam and a whole slew of squares and states from Smolensk to Vladivostok.

But it looks as if Brezhnev's bid for immortality is headed for the dustbin of history. Under a Gorbachev directive, Brezhnev's name has been stripped from all the aforementioned, and the ex-Russian leader is well on his way to becoming Leonid Who.

Let's not tut-tut and cluck-cluck too loudly over this latest example of wretched Russian revisionism. The USSR holds no monopoly on the policy of rewriting history. There used to be, in Southwestern Ontario, an Old World triangle of towns called Paris, London and Berlin. For the past seventy-odd years one of the coordinates has been missing. Paris and London are still there, but Berlin has disappeared, replaced by Kitchener-Waterloo. In a fit of patriotic zeal the name Berlin was banished during World War I.

It ill-behooves Canadians to laugh at the Russian penchant for renaming things when we have a city named after a British-soldier-slash-French-military defeat in which the major annual cultural event is a bratwurst-and-lederhosen Munich import called Oktoberfest.

You never know when the urge to change names is going to appear — or where it will strike. Explorer Martin Frobisher no longer has a town named after him. A few years ago Frobisher Bay officially became Iqaluit. Thunder Bay, my old stomping grounds, did the same thing in 1970. City fathers dropped the names Port Arthur and Fort William, adopting the translation of the traditional Indian name for the place — Thunder Bay.

A few years back, Stalin Township in Ontario renamed itself Hansen Township in honour of a stubborn young Canuck who had the preposterous idea he could make it around the world in a wheelchair. And not so long ago Montreal's famous Dorchester Boulevard became Boulevard René-Lévesque.

Sometimes we get carried away with name changes. Such as the time in the early years of the century when the sensitive citizenry of a certain Canadian prairie town decided their name was too silly and needed to be changed. The town postmaster disagreed. He wrote to the one person in the world he thought might be influential enough to save the town's name. His correspondent returned a thundering volley of several hand-written pages outlining the reasons why a name change would be wrong.

"Forgive me if I write strongly," read the letter, "but this is a matter on which I feel keenly . . . [your] name is an asset, it has no duplicate in the world, [it] draws the feet of young men towards it. Above all, it is the lawful, original, sweat-and-dust-won name of the city, and to change it would be to risk the luck of the city, to disgust and dishearten old-timers, and to advertise abroad the city's lack of faith in itself."

Strong words — and they did the job. The name change was defeated. Which is why today we have a city called Medicine Hat.

Of course the name signed at the bottom of the letter didn't hurt either. Kind of a strange name in itself.

Rudyard Kipling.

Tom Bowdler Rides Again

QUICK, MARTHA, PASS that can of Raid! We've got an infestation of book burners on our hands! It might be funny if it wasn't so blessed depressing, but the fact is we have a group of grown, sentient human beings — a committee of the Toronto Board of Education, no less — that wants to remove the book *Lord of the Flies* from the classroom.

Lord of the Flies, for anyone who's been chained to their TV set for the past quarter century, is about a group of adolescent boys stranded on a tropical island after a plane crash. It's a chilling and riveting account of social unravelling. We watch the kids descend from highly structured British-schoolboy formality to primitive barbarism and ritual murder. I've never met anyone who's read the book and wasn't moved by it. I read it as an adolescent and would count it easily in the top ten of all the books I read growing up. As a matter of fact, I can think of only two books that made more of an impact on me as a young reader: *Tom Sawyer* and *Huckleberry Finn*.

Both of which various school boards have also tried to ban.

The problem is racism — or perceived racism. Huckleberry Finn talks about "the nigger Jim" — which is how he would have been referred to a century ago when the novel was written.

Despite the fact that Jim shows more class and character than anyone else in the book and despite the fact that Mark Twain exposed racists and bigots and the pain they cause in all its ugly detail, the censors' blinkered eyes cannot climb over that word "nigger."

One wonders what they'd do at a Richard Pryor concert.

The case against *Lord of the Flies* is even more suspect. "Nigger," appears 210 times in *Huckleberry Finn*. It appears once in *Lord of the Flies*.

Then of course there's that other racial agitator — William Shakespeare. You and I are very unlikely to see a performance of *Merchant of Venice* ever again because Shakespeare says some very repugnant things about Jews.

Well, here's a news flash — Shakespeare lived nearly 400 years ago. At a time when children, worked like slaves, women were chattel, you could get yourself hanged for stealing a hot-cross bun — and the English hated Jews just because they were Jews.

For some time now, I've kept a copy of a letter to the editor written by a young Guelph, Ontario, student. She wrote in part: "As a recent high school graduate who survived five Shakespearean plays, I plead with authorities to abandon any ideas of censoring Shakespeare or any other great authors studied in high school. William Shakespeare probably was a sexist anti-Semite, as were almost all men of his class and day. But if we do not end this absurd notion of censorship right now, where will it end?"

I don't know where it'll end, but I know what direction we're headed in. Ten of the books most frequently banned by "educators" in the USA are: *The Catcher in the Rye, Of Mice and Men, Nineteen Eighty-Four, Brave New World, Slaughterhouse Five, Black Like Me, One Flew Over the Cuckoo's Nest* and *Deliverance.*

Oh yes, and of course *Lord of the Flies* and *Huckleberry Finn.*

I can't think of a list of ten books I'd rather have my kids read.

Maybe someday we'll get as far as the educator in Leeds, England, who is rewriting our fairy tales to make them more suitable. The Three Bears have been changed to the Three Frogs, so as not to scare little tots. And Goldilocks has been changed to Jackie because it's inappropriate to "glorify a little white girl with blond hair."

The Leeds educator is not alone. In the state schools of Maryland, Tom Sawyer is no longer allowed to say "Honest Injun." He just says "Honest." And in California, an anti-junk-food lobby has seen to it that schoolbooks censor references to ice cream, cake or pie.

A famous man once wrote: "False views do little harm, for everyone takes a salutary pleasure in proving their falseness; and when this is done, one path towards error is closed and the road to truth is often opened."

The writer knew a thing or two about censorship. His name was Charles Darwin.

Well, You Must've Heard the One About . . .

S ORRY I WAS A couple of minutes late. I was being held hostage by some Animal Rights activists who thought my bargain-basement earmuffs were made out of sealskin.

Naw, that's a lie, but give me a chance. I'm practicing. I'm trying to work up an entry for next year's championship playoffs at the Burlington Liars Club.

Burlington, Wisconsin, that is. The club's been around since the 1930s. Its founder and president, Otis Hulett, liked to brag that it was probably the last collection of honest men on the face of the earth. "Everybody is at least a bit of a liar," said Otis, "but we're the only ones who admit it."

Well, the club must have tapped a vein, because over the years more than 97,000 yarn spinners have joined up.

And each year the more ambitious among them submit letters to the club full of preposterous prevarications and breathtaking blarney — all in the hopes of being crowned World Champion Liar. The biggest liar for 1987 was a fellow from Florida who won with a tale about a favourite LP. He played it so much that it got thin enough for him to hear music from both sides of the platter simultaneously. Now I know the beauty of a tall tale is in the telling, but that doesn't sound very funny to me. Heck, I can think of three Canucks down at the local legion who could top that before the beer foam settled. And my old pal Doc Skinner of Thunder Bay — he'd be ashamed to tell a story as pale as that.

Doc was a yarn spinner extraordinaire — actually carried a card identifying him as a certified liar, in case anyone doubted his credentials.

Doc was a fisherman who loved to work the shoals and pools of Gullibility Creek. And his favourite catch was American tourists. Back when he ran a fish camp in Longlac, Doc got tired of giving the same answers to the same dumb tourist questions, so he came up with some more creative ones.

"Say, Doc, how cold does it get up here in Canada in the winter?" Doc would haul out a wooden wall plaque with a small trout on it — a trout that bore a strip of white plush fur down its side. "Well," said Doc, "that's how our fish survive the winter." He also kept a stuffed crow on the store counter — a crow that was dyed brown and had a little papier mâché work around the beak to make it long and needle-like.

"Northern Ontario black fly," Doc would explain straightfaced. "Immature, of course."

Puts me in mind of the story of the Texan and the Calgarian meeting up at the Billionaires Club. Texan looks down at the fellow from Calgary, says: "So, yer from Calgary. Run a few thousan' head o' cattle there, do yuh?"

"No," says the Canadian mildly, "I don't have any cattle."

Texan whacks him on the back, says, "Why, yer like me . . . yew got ahl wells. How many hunderts o' thousan's a barrels yew take out a year?

Calgarian says, "Oh, I don't have any oil wells, either."

"No ahl wells? Well, ya got a spread — ah mean tuh say yew got some land, aincha?"

"Well, yes," says the Calgarian, "I do have six and three-quarter acres."

"Six and three-quarter acres! Hail, in Texas we don't call that a spread. We call that a back yard! Wodda yew call it?"

"Oh, I just call it downtown Calgary."

True story, of course.

Now if you'll excuse me, I've got to look up the address of that club in Burlington, Wisconsin.

Pick a Finger — Any Finger!

WHAT'S YOUR SIGN? Nah, I don't mean Taurus or Capricorn or the guy with the water bucket. I mean, what's your *sign.* Your message. Your personal billboard. Anita O'Hearn has hers picked out. On a clear day you can see it bobbing on the side of a hot-air balloon high over the Walnut Creek Parkway on the outskirts of Los Angeles. The balloon sports a ten-foot-by-twelve-foot photograph of Anita reclining on a red couch, wearing a black velvet dress. The message over the photograph reads: Marry me!!! Interested? Phone 415 555-1758. At age forty-plus, height six feet plus and weight 250 pounds plus, Ms. O'Hearn is not looking for just any wimp who happens to be tootling along the Walnut Creek Parkway — hence the personal sign — a time-honoured approach to a perennial problem.

And signs as advertisements *do* go back a fair way. The oldest one we know of is a Wanted poster dug out of some Theban ruins in Egypt. It offers a reward of "one whole gold coin" for the return of Shem, a runaway slave.

That "want ad" is more than 3,000 years old, and we have no way of knowing whether it was any more effective than Anita O'Hearn's.

What do we know is that people kept using them — signs, I mean. But not signs as we know them. Not signs saying things like Marry Me or Keep Right to Exit Highway 24 South. For most of their history, human signs have not contained words. That's because for most of *our* history, we haven't been able to read. Which is why for a long time most signs were arrows and barber poles and three balls for a pawnshop. That's why pubs and taverns were called things like The Pig and Whistle or The Old Nag. Because even illiterate patrons could recognize a drawing of a pig or a whistle or a broken-down horse and know where they were. (Although they might subsequently forget.)

Funnily enough, we seem to be headed back that way these days — to unworded signs. Highway signs for accommodation, food and fuel now show teepees, knives and forks and gas pumps — not words.

In airports, pictographs of buses and taxis direct you to ground transportation. You follow a drawing of a suitcase to the luggage carousel. And good luck.

But a sign is a sign is a sign — which my dictionary defines as a board, placard or poster displayed in a public place to advertise or to convey information or a direction. But then my dictionary hasn't met the Province of Quebec, where the definition would have to be rewritten to read "a poster displayed in a public place to advertise or to convey information or a direction — in French."

Yeah, Quebec has a whole special, personalized approach to signs. An approach that in any other country would be called censorship. But not in Canada. We're too polite for words like that. We just call it the Sign Law and pretend that it's perfectly normal for government flunkies to ban a language with the stroke of a pen. What we need here is a sign for all our politicians, federal and provincial, who with very few exceptions have bent over forwards to accommodate and appease Quebec's censors. And I believe I've got just the sign. It's a sign that definitely conveys information and direction. Not original, though. Not even among politicians. Matter of fact, a former prime minister once waved this sign to the residents of Salmon Arm, B.C. Sure it's rude. But it's rude in both official languages.

It's Not What You Drive, It's Who You Drive

M Y CAR WOULDN'T start this morning. Which got me thinking a tad negatively about cars in general. Actually, it forced me back inside to phone the Canadian Automobile Association to come and give me a boost. While I waited, I looked up my all-time favourite quote about cars. Comes from a book called *(Perfect) Insolent Chariots*, by John Ketas. Ketas wrote: "The automobile changed our dress, manners, social customs, vacation habits, the shape of our cities, consumer purchasing patterns, common tastes and positions in intercourse."

Yeah, well. It's hard to feel libidinous when you're waiting for the CAA tow-truck.

Ever thought about just how much that filthy, fuming, air-fouling, life-threatening bucket of bolts and spot welds called the automobile has affected our lives? It's killed and disabled more North Americans than any other single agent from lung cancer to world wars, for starters.

Cars desecrate and scarify the countryside into freeways and parking lots, cloverleafs and gas stations, relegate whole nations of cops and commissionaires to writing tickets and manning radar traps, numb the brains of hundreds of thousands of convicts punching out licence plates, who knows how many clerks and sales folk in licence bureaus and used car lots . . . and yet . . .

And yet we love the car. We go into debt to own one, suck up to surly mechanics and skinflint bank managers to keep one. Even bestow our own names on them.

Some folks do, anyway.

Buick? David Dunbar Buick, a turn-of-the-century Scots businessman who moved to Detroit to make cars bearing his name. Henry Ford, of course. Walter Chrysler was another who put his name on wheels. So were Signor Ferrari and Messrs Rolls and Royce.

Karl Benz and Gottfried Daimler were two German carmakers who gave their names to buggies they built.

They even engaged in a kind of automotive cross-pollination. Herr Benz decided to honour the daughter of Herr Daimler by naming a car after her. Which is how we got the Mercedes Benz. Could have been worse. Karl Benz could have opted for the immortalization of his wife. Her name was Bertha.

When you think of it, we've used cars pretty well as far as names go. Visible minorities are represented by Pontiac. The common folk got, well . . . the Volkswagen. Even the yuppies got a piece of the action with the Bricklin and the Delorean. But I doubt that anyone in the history of automotive nomenclature has topped the largely unsung White Manufacturing Company of St. John's, Newfoundland. Here, in its entirety, is the, ahh, advertisement of that firm's latest production model . . . as it appeared in the Births section of the St. John's *Evening Telegram*, a few years back: "The White Production Company announces the 1989 Model Cassandra Madonna White at St. Clare's Mercy Hospital featuring Two-Lung Power, Free Squealing, Bawl Bearings, Water-Cooled Exhaust, Changeable Seat Covers, Water-Spout Overflow. Designer and Chief Engineer Donna White, Advertising Manager Mark White, Technical Assistance Dr. E. Bartellas. Model released at 8:15 P.M. February 6, weight 6 pounds 12 3/4 ounces. This model will be available for display and inspection soon. The management will announce future models from time to time."

All I can say is, congratulations to the staff and management at Whites . . . and Lee Iacocca, eat your carburetor out.

Extra, Extra, Read All about It

E VERY NIGHT on my way home from work I walk past a little wizened white-haired guy who operates one of the last working newsstands that I know of in this part of the world. "All-star final," he croaks. "Washington okays trade deal," or "Million-dollar downtown fire! Getcher all-star final!"

Headlines, he's yelling. Twenty years after McLuhan announces print is dead, here's a guy who yells out newspaper headlines for a living.

Funny thing, headlines. Lester Pearson once told a herd of Parliament Hill newsmen: "Headlines are the only journalistic things that matter. They are, of course," he told the scribblers, "outside your control." Then he added ruefully, "or, so far as I can gather, anybody else's."

Well, sometimes it sure seems that way. Unintentionally hilarious banners like "DEAD POLICEMAN ON FORCE 23 YEARS" and "FARMERS THREATENED BY PLAGUE OF RABBIS" make it seem as if nobody's home in the editorial department.

But sometimes headlines can achieve a kind of inadvertent aptness, too. The one about a circus animal on the loose: "ESCAPED LEOPARD BELIEVED SPOTTED," or that wistful, wishful bold-type entreaty from the fashion pages of a New York paper that read: "FLORIST ASKS GIRLS TO DROP STRAPLESS GOWNS."

But the best newspaper headlines are conscious, crafted works of Art, and I don't know of any paper that does it better than *Variety*, the so-called Hollywood Bible. *Variety* headline writers speak a snappy, pungent shorthand language all their own. *Variety* never uses a twenty-five-cent word where a short, sharp one-syllable jab will win the bout. When the city of Buffalo was paralyzed by a blizzard, *Variety* told the world "BLIZ BOFFS BUFF BIZ." Over a story that analyzed a marked consumer lack of interest in movies with a rural theme, the headline read: "STIX NIX HIX PIX."

Ah, but if you really want to see headlines doing what they're supposed to do — trolling for unsuspecting readers and trying to hook them in the eye, right off the street — I think you have to look to the tabs. The tabloids. Scandal sheets. Supermarket rags.

I spent a half hour in the North Bay airport terminal last week, an airport terminal that is no more interesting than most and duller than one or two.

But not for me. Not this time. I had a rackful of tabloids to stare at.

What a world I found there! You want intergalactic adventure? How about "INJURED UFO CREW IN RUSSIAN HOSPITAL." Health and medicine? "DOCS REMOVE 126-POUND TUMOR FROM 124-POUND GAL." Maybe you like animal stories. Here's one: "63-POUND KITTY EATS PRIZE CHIHUAHUAS." And here's one for Jay over at "Quirks & Quarks": "HUBBY'S 103 MPH SNEEZE BLASTS HAIR OFF WIFE'S HEAD."

My favourite? No contest. I give the nod to the *Weekly World News* headline that goes "2,000-YEAR-OLD MAN FOUND INSIDE TREE." Especially when you take in the subhead that reads "WEARING WATCH THAT'S STILL TICKING."

Sort of the ultimate Timex commercial, I guess. . . .

How about those headlines, though. Did they do their job? Was I compelled to buy the papers and read all about the sixty-three-pound kitty? The UFO crew in Vladivostok General? The woman who must weigh in at minus two pounds?

Buy the papers? Are you kidding? And take the bloom off those great headlines? Besides, I had enough excitement to deal with at the North Bay airport that day. I was en route to Timmins.

F.Y.I.

CRONYMS ARE GREAT. You know — words formed from the first letters of other words? Radar is a good example. Comes from the initials R.A.D.A.R. . . . Radio Detecting And Ranging. "Posslq" is another — standing for Person of Opposite Sex Sharing Living Quarters. Still another is ASAP — As Soon As Possible.

Acronyms crop up everywhere. Down in Chicago 4,000 homes are heated by methane gas. Methane gas derived from cow dung. Supplied by a company called Calorific Recovery Anaerobic Process Incorporated.

Calorific Recovery Anaerobic Process.

You figure out the acronym.

They're all around us, acronyms. Computers? BASIC, a computer language, is an acronym for Beginners All-Purpose Symbolic Instruction Code. B.A.S.I.C. — BASIC.

Medicine? If you ever go to the hospital to visit your grey-haired granny and read LOL in NAD on her chart . . . rest easy. L.O.L. in N.A.D.? That means Little Old Lady in No Apparent Distress.

Some acronyms don't start off as words. They're just abbreviations. But we use them so much they become words. Short forms like FBI . . . DOA . . . 747. We get 'em from sports — TD, ERA, MVP; we get 'em from politics — NDP, GST; we get 'em from work — CBC, CTV; and from non-work — UIC. We get acronyms and abbreviations from all over the place, but I don't know if there's any single agency that supplies more than the Canadian military.

I spent eight days in Lahr and Baden Solingen not long ago. Eight days in which I learned not to say "Say what?" when someone spoke of RSMs and PMQs, OCs and COs. RSM is a Regimental Sergeant Major. PMQ is Private Married Quarters. OC is Officer Commanding (Major). CO is Commanding Officer (Lieutenant Colonel). See what I mean? EMDW — Elementary, My Dear Watson.

Listening to a couple of members of the Canadian Forces shoot the breeze is a bit like eavesdropping on a conversation between Martians.

They say things like, "So he asked the SSM if he can take a C4 with him . . . up in the CF 18! Well, naturally, when the RSM hears about it he's on to NDHQ. By this time the DNDOI gets wind of it and blammo! The ya'alls get into the act. And that's when the SHTF."

This kind of talk is tough for a civilian to follow.

I asked one of our helpful guides in Lahr, a Capt. Reid Campbell, if the blizzard of letters and acronyms didn't get confusing — even for a vet like him. He thought for a moment and said, "Well, yes. I remember being mystified once. I came up to a door with a title on it . . . had no idea what it stood for. I tried to work the letters out. Liaison Auxilliary Defence Instruction Executive Staff . . . nah. Maybe Lateral Ancillary Department of Information Engineering Station? I didn't think so. How about Logistical Armaments Deployment Inter Echelon Squadron? I knew that was wrong," he said. And then the captain just stopped talking.

I couldn't stand the suspense. "Well, what was it?" I asked him. "L.A.D.I.E.S. — what did it stand for?"

Captain Campbell made that peculiar Canadian military gesture I saw so much in West Germany — his index finger encircling his nose. "Beats me," he said.

PART 4
The Places We Go

United We Fly

JUST OCCURRED TO ME that lately I've been spending more time in airports than I care to. Not that airports by themselves bother me all that much. My hangup is the traditional method we have of getting from airport to airport. Fear of flying is what I've got.

Well, that's not exactly true, either. I'm pretty well used to flying. My big character flaw is fear of crashing. It starts to show up in the airport waiting lounge. I begin asking myself silly questions like . . . well, take the security scanners. Given that I have to spread-eagle in front of a wand-wielding rent-a-tyrant and try to justify having a metal zipper in my pants, how does a guy with a steel plate in his head ever get through? And other questions like . . . could a pilot, if he was really bored or drunk, or if he had, say, a loose steel plate in his head . . . could he put a 747 through an Immelman turn? Pilots don't have to go through the scanners, of course.

My uneasiness doesn't ease any when I'm finally inside that metal pipe, strapped down like Gulliver into a seat clearly intended for a pre-schooler, being lectured about "loss of cabin pressure," "flotation devices under my seat" and the possibility of "slight turbulence" by immaculately groomed androids with stunningly insincere smiles.

Some people have no such reservations about airplanes. Some folks are quite the opposite. Some folks are charter members of the Mile High Club, which is to say they have, ah, cemented their bond with a fellow club initiate in the most graphic and intimate way in an airplane at an altitude at or exceeding 5,280 feet above sea level.

Yes, friends, while you and I are white-knuckling our plastic chair tables or trying fruitlessly to wrench the tops off those overpriced perfume bottles of hootch, the passengers in 18B and 18C are both in 18A.

Just such a couple joined the Mile High Club recently on American Airlines flight 37 from Zurich to San Diego.

Actually this one was a little messier than most initiations. Apparently the flight attendants took umbrage and tried to interrupt the ceremony. This understandably vexed the devotees and also some folks across the aisle — "voyeurs" the airline lawyer dubbed them; I prefer to think of them as a rooting section. By the time the plane touched down for a Chicago stopover, there were police cars with winking lights all over the tarmac.

Far as I'm concerned the whole thing is a clear misunderstanding. That couple never should have been on an American Airlines flight.

They were obviously meant to fly United.

A Capital Capital

OTTAWA . . . autumn . . . so this is it. The Nation's Capital. Birthplace of notions as various as nuclear subs for the Arctic, the Museum of Civilization, the Ottawa Senators, the disembowelment of Via Rail.

Funny . . . *seems* like a sensible enough place.

Ottawa. Ontario. Canada. Latitude forty-five degrees, twenty-four minutes north, Longitude seventy-five degrees, forty-three minutes west, tucked into a crook of the Ottawa River as it truckles down from the height of land to the broad St. Lawrence.

The town was named in 1855, after an Indian tribe. It was chosen as the country's capital two years later by Queen Victoria, who, sitting in a damp and drafty London drawing room, pointed a pudgy finger at the name Ottawa among five Canadian urban contenders and pronounced, "That is the place."

And so it is — Ottawa: the nation's capital.

But not always smoothly. Ottawa has its detractors, you know.

"Dullsville on the Rideau," Fotheringham, the Southam churl, once called it. "A cultural desert," sniffed Judy LaMarsh. A turn-of-the-century literary pit bull by the name of Goldwyn Smith snarled that Ottawa was "a sub-Arctic lumber village converted by royal mandate into a political cockpit." Writer Ronald Lee was a little less venomous. He pronounced Ottawa "a strange city . . . you can't love it, as you do Montreal, but you can't hate it, as you do Toronto." I think the poet Alden Nowlan probably got closest to the essence of the place. "The first thing you learn here," wrote Nowlan, "is that the country bears the same relationship to the government that outer space bears to earth."

There's one thing that makes Ottawa unique: no main industry. Ottawa is a government town. Asking Ottawa for its GNP is like asking for a eunuch's next of kin.

In Ottawa, the streets are unusually clean. The buildings are unnaturally spiffy and well scrubbed. And the suits . . . the suits . . . are everywhere. You can spot a herd of muskox by its characteristic defensive circle. A flock of Canada geese by its raggedy V formation. Ottawa denizens travel in small, irregular clusters of suits, each suit clutching an attaché case and uttering that distinctive Ottawa cry: "Taxi! Taxi!"

Ah, but that familiar bedrock of Canadian uncertainty is alive and well in Bytown. A radio host opens an interview with an out-of-towner by saying, "Well, how about it — did our beautiful city live up to your expectations?" Uh, expectations? I suspect only politicians come to Ottawa with expectations — and only the gormless politicians at that. But, beautiful? No doubt about it. It would be hard for a city *not* to be beautiful with the most stunning architecture in the country; a Caesar's tribute worth of paintings and sculptures; the smoky Gatineaus in the distance; and the Rideau and the Ottawa doing their silver embroidery right through the midsection of town.

As for that other . . . fourth . . . dimension of Ottawa, well, the Welsh writer Jan Morris got there first. I imagine her leaning out the balcony of her suite in the Château Laurier, looking and musing, then going back inside to write: "Half a continent looks towards Ottawa for its leadership — millions of square miles are centred upon those very buildings on the hill . . . from Niagara to the Northwest Passage the mandate of this city runs. Now that," wrote Morris, "is awesome."

And she's right. It is. It really is.

Ahh . . . Saltspring

WHEN YOU PAY a visit to the magical kingdom of Saltspring, you have to be prepared for a certain degree of, um, eccentricity. First of all, you are still in Canada, even though the city of Vancouver is to your east, the city of Victoria to the south, and there's not a hockey arena to be seen.

Then there's the island itself. At the extreme northern tip, you'll find . . . Southey Point. Down towards the nether end you run into Mount Maxwell, where a sasquatch may or may not have carried off a young damsel many years ago. (She went for a walk, and all they ever found was her hankie and a large, bare footprint.)

And in between Mount Maxwell and Southey Point, some of the most mythical and evocative place names this side of a road production of *Brigadoon*. Vesuvius Harbour, the town of Ganges, Walkers Hook, Maracaibo, the Trincomali Pass, Burgoyne Bay . . .

All this on a gobbet of vaulting, roller-coaster turf that's only twenty miles long and six miles across. You can tootle around it in a Honda in a half hour without ever getting into high gear. High gears are kind of useless on Saltspring — in cars and in people. I don't know if it's the island that Time forgot or the other way around — that Saltspringers forgot Time. I do know that I overheard a conversation in a restaurant there that went like this:

"Hey Arvid, what day is it?"

"Ummmmmm, Monday, I think."

"Nope, can't be Monday. I remember Monday."

"Oh? You think Wednesday, maybe?"

"No. No, it must be Tuesday cause the Driftwood paper just came out. It always comes out Tuesdays."

And these were Saltspring Island businesspeople!

They just don't give a damn about time out on Saltspring. I met a real estate agent there who doesn't wear a wristwatch! "I just took it off one day," he said. "Never had a good reason to put it back on."

They don't give a damn about a lot of things out there on Saltspring. Fashion trends . . . cost-efficiency ratios . . . keeping up with the Joneses. I met one refugee from France there — a baker by the name of Pascal — who doesn't even believe in indoor plumbing. He's got a galvanized bathtub in his back yard. Whenever he wants a hot bath he fills the tub with cold water and lights a fire under it. Told a story about it while I was there — with all the appropriate Gallic fatalism. "Las' night," says Pascal, "I feel the bat'tob op weeth watair . . . light ze fire . . . mah wafe and I are seet in eet weeth a glass of wine . . . we look op ze starrrs . . . and eet begeen to snow."

Well, yeah, it does snow on Saltspring Island (it is Canada, after all) — but not often, and certainly not for long. Still, can you imagine how swell it must have been in that bathtub, even in a snowstorm . . . a glass of wine in your hand . . . your sweetie down at the other end . . . the embers of a woodfire warming your buns . . . looking up into the Saltspring night sky, trying to figure out exactly where the house lights on the hills leave off and the stars begin.

I'm going back. I have to go back. Well, I want to see how that half-finished totem pole in Fulford Harbour is coming along. I want to see if the folks who live in that teepee by St. Mary's Lake actually do get mail delivery. And anyway, I have to go find my wristwatch. I . . . took it off out there someplace.

Didn't miss it till I got back home.

Sayonara, Banff

T HE FIRST SNOWFALL of winter is an important occasion for
Canadians — it's the last time most of us have a good word to
say about the White Stuff. Let Californians burble on about White
Christmases and winter wonderland fantasies; any Canuck with a
few kilometres on his toboggan knows that winter is mostly a hard
slog, and unrelieved white is a decorator shade that gets pretty
dreary after a month or two. Still and all, that first snowfall is nice
and decidedly magical. Which is why it's good if you can arrange
to be somewhere special to see it.

I'm set for the winter this year — I saw my first snowfall in the
most spectacular setting this country affords: deep in the Alberta
Rockies. Banff, to be precise.

Am I the last Canadian in the land to discover this national
treasure? Possibly. The people I met there couldn't believe I'd
managed to pass four and a half decades without seeing the place.
For anyone else who's neglected their patriotic duty, I offer a
thumbnail sketch.

Actually, sketching Banff on a thumbnail would be like playing
Beethoven's Ninth on a police whistle. The place is, to reclaim a
word from schoolyard hipsters, awesome. It's a dot on a ripple of
earth's crust that exploded up and outward millions of years ago.

Did I say "ripple"? That's a touch understated. The tortured
peaks and gouged-out valleys that surround Banff are sculpted on
a scale calculated to remind the average human being of his
puniness. The sheer crags thrust up, up, like massive ocean waves,
frozen in mid-curl. Clumps of rugged conifers straggle up the
mountain flanks, then trail away, peter out, surrendering to barren

granite and finally, snow so high that it never melts. Look up to the top and see clouds disemboweling themselves on the jagged peaks. Look down at inlaid orbs like Lake Louise and Moraine Lake — jewels of glacial water so unnaturally green that it makes the breath snag in the throat.

Hang around Banff National Park too long and you run the risk of developing a permanently rubber neck.

The town of Banff itself is clean and pleasant with a sufficiency of decent restaurants and enough shopping opportunities to sate the lusts of Imelda Marcos. The goodies range from junky ninety-nine-cent key chains to furs, jewels and jade sculpture, five grand and up. But it's not the range of merchandise that strikes the first-time visitor to Banff — it's the signs in the stores. Banff is a fluently bilingual town.

English and Japanese.

The Japanese come to Banff by the thousands every year. They come to get married, to ski, to shop, to hold conventions. They come in pairs and in planeloads. And they spend an awful lot of money while they're here.

"Banff is their Niagara Falls," a long-time resident told me.

It's also their Dallas. One of the most popular Japanese television soap operas is shot amidst the stately splendour of the Banff Springs Hotel.

The Japanese presence is very strong in Banff. There's a traditional Japanese restaurant downtown, many of the stores and hotels are owned and operated by Japanese and those that aren't usually have at least one Japanese-speaking staff member.

Which can lead to a certain amount of confusion. A pleasant woman by the name of Yuki at the hotel check-in desk apologized profusely to me in charming, if somewhat stilted, English. She just couldn't find any record of my reservation. Hoping to help, I looked over her shoulder at the computer screen.

And discovered Yuki was searching for a Mr. Brack.

Does it cause any tension, this Japanese presence in Banff? None that I could detect. That evening when the first snow of the season came tumbling down in plump flakes, bleaching the lawns and mantling the mountains, the Japanese trooped outside like the rest of us, whooping, making snowballs awkwardly, shrieking at the perverse delight of cold snow down the neck. We were all kids again.

Some of the faces were a little more coppery, that's all.

Winnie the White River Pooh

IF I WAS A RESIDENT of White River, Ontario, I think I'd be wondering about now if my town was afflicted with a case of giant municipal B.O. For some reason, White River can't buy, rent or lease an ounce of respect.

It's a mystery to me. I've been to White River. It's a perfectly respectable hamlet on the Trans Canada highway, well placed to serve as a pit stop or a wayside rest for anyone who wants a break from jousting with tractor trailers while driving over the north of Superior hump between Thunder Bay and Sault Ste. Marie. Lovely scenery, great fishing, friendly folks — so how come White River gets such shoddy treatment?

First we give it the archival cold shoulder. Can't find White River in the *Canadian Encyclopedia*. Oh, there's room in there for Whitehorse and White Rock and Whiteshell. We included Bob White and Whitefish and White Paper and even White-collar Crime — but White River? Not so much as a preposition.

Then there was the famous White River thermometer — a huge neon billboard by the side of the highway that showed a thermometer festooned with icicles and just a tiny dot of mercury at the bottom. "Welcome to White River," said the legend — "coldest spot in Canada." Stood there for years. People used to take pictures of each other beside that thermometer. You could even buy postcards that showed it.

Then some officious nitpicker in Environment Canada took issue with the White River claim. Said the record wasn't official. The thermometer came down.

You would think that the bear might have succeeded where the *Canadian Encyclopedia* and the neon thermometer failed. You would think surely the bear could put White River on the map. The bear is historical. Goes back to World War I when a Canadian Army lieutenant passing through White River bought a live bear cub from a hunter for $20. He took the bear with him to England. When he found out he was heading for the trenches, the lieutenant gave the bear to the London zoo.

The bear, named Winnipeg by the homesick Canadian soldier, became a star at the London zoo. And nobody loved him more than a little toddler by the name of Chris Milne, even though his preschool tongue had trouble pronouncing the name Winnipeg. Little Christopher just called the bear "Winnie." Fortunately for little Christopher, his father was a writer. Fortunately for all of us, actually. Chris's father was A. A. Milne. He wrote the world-famous Winnie the Pooh books and immortalized the little cub from White River.

Now you would think being the hometown of the most famous bear in English literature would be enough to earn White River a little respect. Town officials thought so, too. They were all set to put up a big statue of Winnie, until the letter from Walt Disney Studios arrived. Disney holds the copyright to Winnie the Pooh. The Disney lawyers said no dice. No statue. Period. So here we have an American owner of a British work saying that Canadians cannot honour an Ontario bear with a Manitoba name.

Free Trade. How do you like it so far?

Fabulous Fredericton

ONE OF THE BEAUTIES of this country of ours is that it is so vast and so varied that there is just no danger of ever running out of magical spots. I stumbled on a new one last week. The city of Fredericton, New Brunswick.

Now, don't ask me how I managed to get to middle age without ever setting foot in Fredericton. I don't know. All I do know is I'm glad I discovered it before *old* age body-slammed me to the living room chesterfield. This way, I figure I've got a good twenty or twenty-five years' worth of conniving to figure out how to get back to Fredericton for something longer than a weekend.

I was down in Fredericton for a speaking engagement, and it should have been a slam-bam, in-and-out, hit-and-run affair. Airport to hotel, quick shower and change, off to dinner, make speech, back to hotel and out on the first morning flight. But it didn't work that way. There was something about Fredericton, something about those stately, impeccably maintained 200- and 300-year-old houses, something about the improbably wide Saint John River lazily undulating right past the downtown area, something about the mellow amiability of the place that told me it would be a mistake to just jump in and jet out of Fredericton without a bit of a look round.

So I stayed in Fredericton for the weekend and I discovered a lot of things — the process called Aitkenization, for one thing. Anybody who didn't know that Max Aitken, a.k.a. Lord Beaverbrook, hailed from Fredericton before they hit the city limits, would certainly know it before they left town. There is a statue of the chap in the centre of town. There is also a Beaverbrook Art Gallery, a Beaverbrook Theatre, a Beaverbrook Reading Room, a Beaverbrook Birdbath. I know. I could see most of them from the window of my hotel. The Lord Beaverbrook Hotel, of course.

Whatever his purpose, Max Aitken gave Fredericton a leg up on similar Canadian communities. The population of Fredericton is only about 50,000, but it has all the aforementioned amenities as well as a full-fledged university. How many other small Canadian cities have that kind of cultural clout?

Sounding a little too hoity-toity for your taste? Fredericton's got the antidote for that. It's called the Boyce Farmers Market. It happens every Saturday morning in downtown Fredericton.

At the market you can buy anything from handcrafted lawn furniture to garden manure to Jersey milk with the cream still on top, to Acadian quilts, used books, melt-in-your-mouth pastries, cheeses beyond imagination. I could go on, but I don't have to because the Boyce Farmers Market does, every Saturday morning, summer and winter.

At the market you will also have the chance to meet Goofy Roofy. Actually, you will have no choice in the matter. As soon as Goofy Roofy finds out you're from out of town she will grab you by the arm, waltz you into her restaurant and sit you down, sometimes with total strangers. Doesn't matter. No one's a stranger long at Goofy Roofy's. Word of warning, though. The proprietress is a bit of a CBC Radio fanatic — as you will divine from the menu. Two of the specials are Smoked Gzowski and Ben's Wick.

Fredericton seems to be good at turning out oddballs who turn out to have more on the ball than the rest of us. People like not-so-goofy Ruth Chappel, Max Aitken . . . and Richard Hatfield, ex-premier and one of the most fascinating politicians this country's ever produced. Mr. Hatfield once explained his fondness for travel by saying, "I was elected to *run* New Brunswick. No one said I had to *live* there."

He was, as usual, pulling our leg. Mr. Hatfield lived in a modest cottage-y home, behind a forest of no-doubt deliberately tacky lawn ornaments . . . right in the heart of Fredericton.

Mr. Hatfield's gone now, but his hometown lives on. Go see it. It's worth it.

One Man's Camp Is Another Man's Cottage

WE GAS A LOT about the "true North" here in the Great White You-Know-What, but the truth is, we can't even agree on what North is. Is Parry Sound in the north? Compared to Pangnirtung? What about Barrie?

Well, I can't speak to the national scene but when it comes to telling North from South in Ontario I've got a rule of thumb that's more reliable than an Eagle Scout compass rolled up in a CAA road map.

Flag down the next native you see and ask him where he spends his summer holidays.

If he says, "at camp," you're in the north. If he says, "at the cottage," you're in the nether regions of Ontari-ari-ari-o.

In suburban Toronto, where I grew up, it was always "cottage." You "went to the cottage" for the weekend. You spent your summers "up at the cottage." You caught your big bass "off the dock at Grandpa's cottage."

Camps? Sure, we knew camps. There were Bible camps, Boy Scout camps, Indian camps and Van Camp's pork and beans.

I didn't hear an adult refer to any other kind of camp until I was in my mid-thirties and an ex-Hogtowner-cum-greenhorn newly settled in Thunder Bay.

I remember the moment well. I was getting to know my next-door neighbour, a laconic Finn, over a pot of coffee. He hoisted his mug, took a hearty slurp and then said, "Nagst summer, you comink to our camp for veekent."

Oh dear, I said to myself. What have I moved in next to? A religious fundamentalist? A Nordic Baden-Powell?

Nothing of the sort. Old Yorma was extending the ultimate in northern neighbourliness — an invitation to spend a weekend at his summer place.

Not that a northerner's camp and a southerner's cottage are interchangeable. By and large the northern camp is a good deal rougher and readier than its effete southern cousin. Northerners go to camp for the fishing, the hunting and the solitude — not to play a series of Away Games in the Keeping Up with the Jones Tournament. You'll see none of your sleek teak and mahogany Ditchburns or Greavette Streamliners lashed to a cleat in front of a northern camp. More likely it'll be a fourteen-foot dinged-in, bunged-up Lund aluminum runabout with a red stripe down its flank. Camp owners tilt towards workhorse boats. Sluggers that can handle everything from uncharted shoals and new-this-year beaver dams to submerged deadheads and premature feeze-ups that put an unexpected half inch of skim ice on the lake.

The camps themselves are far less prettified than the enchanted rustic fantasies you often find in the Muskokas or the Haliburton Highlands. I don't remember seeing too many geranium planters or driveways lined with kitschy painted rocks at camps around the Lakehead. Flagpoles are scarce up there, and so are boat-houses, gazebos and guest cabins.

So which is better, the camp or the cottage? Don't ask this tainted witness. I was brought up on cottages and weaned on camps. I still get tears in my eyes recalling the smell of a Muskoka cottage newly opened in spring . . . two parts kerosene to one part moth-ball, with a pinch of pine resin and a sprinkle of mouse poop tossed in for seasoning.

On the other hand, I have experienced few finer moments than one I recall sitting on a porch overlooking Lake Superior, watching the bronzed globe of a sinking sun get upstaged by a family of cavorting loons.

Camps and cottages, cottages and camps. They both have their warts and their beauty spots. The season is shorter for camps — and fiercer. The bugs are merciless up north. Only a neophyte or a masochist would venture out to camp unarmed with a bottle of Off, Flit, Musk Oil or (a northern icon) McKirdy's Special Repelfly.

Southern Ontario cottages are much more benign — and don't try to frighten me with sagas of mosquitos in Muskoka. Compared to Northern Ontario blackflies, they are lap gerbils.

You get fewer surprises at cottages. Such as looking out your kitchen window straight into the beady black button eyes of a foraging momma black bear *avec famille* promenading along your front porch.

On the other hand, northern camps are accessible. Lots of camp owners simply move to their camps for the summer and commute to work. It's only an extra half hour or so. No northerner I know would believe the three-, four- and five-hour chrome-crunching, fender-bending odysseys many Southern Ontarians brave to get to and from their cottages.

Cottage or camp . . . camp or cottage.

I don't care what you call it, I don't have either, and it's been a long hard winter and I can't wait to be invited to one.

Or the other.

Blue-eyed Weasels
from Hell

THE FIRST THING that strikes an out-of-town viewer, standing at the starting gate that is on the shores of Great Slave Lake, which still sports a six-foot-thick blanket of ice on this the first weekend in April — the first thing that strikes your effete shivering Southern Ontarian greenhorn is . . . *the dogs.* This is the annual Canadian Championship Dog Derby here. The city of Yellowknife has been hosting this sled race and drawing the best dog mushers in the world since 1955. Over the next three days these dogs, harnessed into platoons of anywhere from five to nine members, will try to haul big wooden sleds and their bigger, parka-muffled owners over 150 miles of frozen ice and snow.

And these dogs . . . *do not look up to the job.* You remember the On, King!, Sergeant Preston of the Yukon, *Call of the Wild* type huskies that we grew up with? The ones that were the size of a chesterfield, stared down entire wolf packs and could pick up small glaciers in their teeth? Well, these dogs ain't them.

The sled dogs at this year's Yellowknife dog derby are not much bigger than fox terriers. They don't have that icy, make-my-day stare or that clear-the-track presence of your classic husky. If it came to first dibs on the Doctor Ballard, I'm not sure they could take my cat. These are racing dogs, a Yellowknifer explains to me, purposely bred for their small size and weight. Another more traditional spectator snorts, spits and grumbles, "I call them racing weasels with blue eyes." Whatever . . . they don't look like sled dogs to me.

Ahh, but Wayne Gretzky doesn't look like a hockey player, either, until he gets the puck. When the black powder rifle is fired to start the race, the baying blue-eyed weasels from Hell lay their ears flat, lunge into their traces and take off. They cover fifty miles each day for three straight days. And they do it whether it's forty below or there are puddles on the ice. Whether it's clear and sunny or a full-bore blizzard.

Did I mention tough? One of the dogs runs the entire race sporting an incongruous blue bootee on one paw to protect a cut. One of the mushers lugs an extra burden, too. He's fighting a bout of pneumonia.

Yellowknife's annual dog derby doesn't get a lot of national attention — even though there's $30,000 in prize money, even though it's about 30,000 times more exciting than most curling matches or any Leafs game. It's a pity more Canadians don't get to see the race because it's thrilling, it's spectacular and it's all Canadian — well, almost all Canadian. This year's first and second places were won by American dog teams.

But the dog derby is nothing if not democratic. You don't have to be Canadian to win. Or male, come to that. This year two of the mushers who went the 150-mile distance were women. When one of them stood up at the awards banquet that night, there was an audible gasp from the crowd. I think a lot of us were realizing for the first time that under all those layers of parka and sealskin mitts and wind pants there had been a very beautiful woman who didn't look the least bit like the Mad Trapper of Rat River. The fellow sitting next to me was particularly smitten. Oh, boy, I thought. I hope he doesn't whistle or thump on the table or yell something stupid and sexist like woo-woo or hubba-hubba. He watched her through eyes like pie plates, then murmured reverently. "Oh, man! That Kristen. She's got such grrrrreat dogs."

Wanted: One Car Salesman

S HOW A LITTLE RESPECT, eh? A close friend of mine is at death's door — which means that one day very soon I'm going to have to do something that I hate.

Worse than going to the dentist.

Worse than filling out my income tax form.

Worse than sitting through a session of Question Period, even.

Okay, you're right — I'm being melodramatic. Heck, it's not even a close friend that's dying. It's my car, and it's been ill for some time. Truth to tell, it's seven years old, baffed out, caved in, used up and run down. It's got a cracked windshield, uncountable dings in the hood and fenders, an exhaust system that sounds like the soundtrack from *Apocalypse Now* and a spare tire with less tread than a newborn's backside. My province's lavish applications of road salt have left my buggy looking like an Iraqi oil platform after a U.S. attack. Its odometer registers more kilometres than the Telstar satellite. The monthly repair bills required to keep my heap on the road have now reached — nay, surpassed — the monthly payments I made when it was new.

In short, my car deserves to die.

But that's not my problem. My problem is that its impending demise thrusts me into the dreaded dilemma I hinted at above. Which is to say . . .

I'm going to have to visit a car lot.

And I hate it! I hate the flocks of snow-white, tooth-capped, eye-wincing insincere smiles that await me. I hate the bone-crushing handshakes, the mood music, the "Call me Al, Art — I can call you Art, can't I?" introductions. I hate the inevitable, unavoidable

118

conversations about fuel consumption ratios, double wishbone suspensions, power train warranties and pro-rated financing options. I understand none of this, of course, but I'm too chicken-hearted to say so, so I stand in the showroom, kicking tires and nodding enthusiastically until somebody in a plaid jacket steers me to a chair and shows me where to sign.

I hate all of it.

Which maybe explains why I think I love John Price. John Price is a knight in Turtle-waxed armour for a terminal carlotophobic like me. He even looks kind of knightly with his Man from Glad silver pompadour, his custom-tailored suit and his Rolex watch, grinning confidently behind the wheel of his burgundy Alfa Romeo. He might pass for an aging tennis pro or perhaps a matinee idol from the heyday of Hollywood, but no, that's not what John Price does.

John Price buys cars. For the fun of it.

Well, not exactly. He buys cars for the fun of it and for the profit in it, too. For 10 per cent of the amount he saves off the sticker price plus $100, John Price will buy your next car for you — and he guarantees you'll get the best deal in town.

"I love matching wits with car dealers," says Price. "I know how much profit is built into the sticker price and I know how low they're willing to come."

It's beautiful. John Price knows more about the cars he buys than the salesmen he buys them from. You phone him up and tell him what kind of car you want — the make, the colour, the options — and he goes out and gets it for you. He offers the dealer only a few hundred dollars over the dealer's cost. And the smart dealers take it, because they know that John Price will be back again and again and again. And little commissions add up.

John Price will even nurse his clients through the paperwork of buying a car. He holds your hand while the financial arrangements are made, breaks the warranty agreement down into basic English and answers all those questions that you're afraid to ask the dealer.

I know what you're thinking. You're thinking, "What's the matter with this schlemiel? His car is dying, he needs a new car, he's too gutless or witless to buy one himself, so why doesn't he phone up John Price and hire him to find a new set of wheels?"

There's just one small problem.

John Price is a dream come true to would-be car buyers all right — but only if they live west of the San Andreas Fault. He lives in San Francisco — which is about 2,627 miles, 787 yards farther than I would care to trust my mortally stricken vehicle to carry me.

Hmmmm.

I wonder if John Price makes house calls?

How I Spent
My Vacation

W E DIDN'T GET SICK. I want to stress that right off the top, because everyone who heard we were going south for a quick winter vacation rolled their jealousy-raddled eyes and hinted darkly that we'd soon be convulsed in the throes of Caribbean Quickstep or Bahama Trauma or worse.

Didn't happen. And why should it? This was no nineteenth-century trek up the Zambesi. We were simply hopping down to Miami, then catching a short island flight to a small tropical atoll — one of the jewels in the Bahamian archipelago that sprawls like a discarded necklace just off the coast of Florida.

"I wouldn't check my bags right through if I were you," counselled the check-in agent at the Toronto airport. "Better to pick them up at your Miami stopover and re-check them for the island flight".

Didn't *The Rime of the Ancient Mariner* start off something like that?

Miami airport turns out to be a high-tech maze of "concourses" and "satellite terminals" loosely blanket-stitched together with tunnels and walkways and shuttle buses. When we arrive we have just twenty-nine minutes to hunt down our luggage, re-check it and find our connecting flight to the Bahamas. In accordance with the immutable Third Law of St. Jude, Patron Saint of Lost Travellers, we discover that our luggage, our point of departure and our bodies are as separated from one another as is physically possible without leaving Dade County.

Somehow we do it, and arrive at Satellite Terminal 12-H sweating, gasping, with three minutes to spare before our flight to the island is scheduled to depart.

The key word there is "scheduled." Fifteen minutes elapse. A half hour.

"Any idea when flight 112 will be leaving?" an erstwhile passenger inquires with admirable Canadian diffidence.

"Soon as I can find a pilot," says the dispatcher. Oh yes. A pilot. Good idea. One hour passes. A pilot is found. Passengers are herded out on the tarmac to what looks like a kayak with wings. Nine passengers and the recently discovered pilot will attempt to board this craft and defy gravity over 150 miles of shark-infested water not terribly far from the Bermuda Triangle.

Actually, you don't "board" this plane. You "don" it. Like a body stocking.

The passengers include your correspondent, his increasingly thin-lipped Lifetime Companion, a brace of equally overheated prepubescents and one Piltdown-size cigar-chomping gent who looks like a Sumo wrestler gone to seed. The kids are stowed at the back "just so we can get off the ground," the pilot explains guilelessly. The rest of us winnow our way into the fuselage while the Sumo wrestler squeezes into the seat next to the pilot.

You know . . . where the co-pilot usually sits?

Never mind, it's only a short flight, and the addition of a co-pilot would probably mean one of us would have to make the trip lashed to a wheel strut. Pre-flight jitters are premature in any case, because when Sumo attempts to adjust his seat, a fist-size chunk of steel pings across the cockpit like shrapnel. The seat is broken. We must taxi to a hangar for repairs.

Eventually the seat is fixed, the plane gets off the ground and drones 150 miles due east to fetch up finally on a short runway scraped out of the mangrove and coral of one of the smaller Bahamian cays. We deplane, grab our bags and taxi to the hotel, scarcely five hours late.

At last. Now let the pampering begin.

I tell them who I am, the fact that I am a writer here to do a story on their fabled isle and that I am ready to claim the luxury villa that the Bahamas Ministry of Tourism has so graciously reserved for me.

I am received with a look much like the one the Arawak Indians must have bestowed on Columbus when he stumbled ashore on these islands almost five centuries ago.

There is no reserved villa. There is no reservation. They have never heard of me.

But what about my contact here? The public relations director I was told would meet me at the airport and escort me to the hotel? Elliot — yes, that's it! Let me speak to Elliot, dammit!

"Ain't no Elliot here. Used to be, long time ago. He's in Foat Lawduhdale now."

Perhaps it's Christian charity. Perhaps it's simple pity. Or maybe it's the Bank of Montreal MasterCard plus three pieces of identification I produce — whatever, they give us a room. It is not a swell room, but it beats the winged kayak back at the airstrip. The next two days are spent assuring the nervous hotel manager that we are not a pair of bunko artists fast-talking our way through a free holiday.

"Just call up the Bahamas Ministry of Tourism in Nassau," I soothe. "They're picking up the tab. We're their guests."

It is not, alas, that easy. Telephone service in the Caribbean is just a kind of rough concept. You dial half a number and the line goes dead. Sometimes — rarely — you actually get through and establish contact with someone at the other end. Then the line goes dead. You dial again. And again. And again.

Finally, miraculously, we do get through to the ministry. Yes, praise God, they have heard of this junket. They are devastated that things have not gone well. They will make up for it tomorrow, when we fly to Nassau. There will be a lavish luncheon and we are to be the guests of honour! We will be given an escorted tour of the city. Then we will be taken to our overnight accommodation at a splendid five-star villa where reservations for dinner have already been made.

You don't want to hear how the plane wasn't at the airstrip. How it didn't arrive at the airstrip for four hours. How, when it did arrive, it blew a tire. How there were no spare tires at the airstrip and we had to wait for one to be flown in.

From Nassau, of course.

To keep a long and ghastly saga short and bittersweet: we get to Nassau too late for the luncheon, too late for the tour, but in time, if we hurry, to honour our dinner reservations at the restaurant "attached to our hotel complex," the lady from the Tourist Board had explained.

123

To be fair, the villa was gorgeous in the setting sun with bougainvillea trailing over the private patio and almost into the private pool. Lifetime Companion softens, even offers a grim smile. We might, I think to myself, pull this one out yet.

"Why don't you have a shower?" I croon. "I'll mosey down to the hotel office and find out what time they serve dinner."

Which I do. Only to find the office closed. Locked. Lights out. No sign of life, recent or imminent. Only a note tacked to a fence near the door that reads:

"Office Closed. For emergency or after hours go to Villa 8."

I find Villa 8. It, too, seems deserted and lifeless. I push on a wooden door leading to the patio. It swings creakily, the kind of door that would have delighted Alfred Hitchcock. "Hellooooo," I cry. "Anybody home?"

"COME IN!" screeches a fishwifey voice. At this point a dog that looks like a carpet slipper with teeth comes scrabbling around the corner yapping and yipping.

"Ahh . . . my name is Arthur Black and I j —"

Yapyapyap

"COME IN . . . HELLO!"

"Ah, yes ma'am, thank you. I just wond — ahh, your dog . . ."

Yipyipyip

"HELLO . . . COME IN!"

Why doesn't she come out, I hiss to myself, glowering and shaking my fist at the dog. The dog yaps on and so do I, stammering apologies and explanations and asking for directions to the restaurant.

"HELLO . . . COME IN!" says the voice mindlessly. So I do. I bunt the dog aside with my foot, open the door and peer in to find . . .

A parrot. For the past five minutes I have been conversing with a large Blue-fronted Amazon parrot.

On the plus side, our villa did offer a mini-bar in the bedroom. Which was good, because we never did find the restaurant. But we made do on Planters Peanuts and lukewarm cans of club soda. By this time food was a distant thirteenth on our list of Lifetime Priorities. Number-one concern was Getting the Hell Home.

The night was spent lying on our backs, listening to the drone of the air conditioner and worrying about our supposed early morning flight. Did I mention that our villa had no telephone? It didn't. Our guide had promised to have a taxi waiting at the door at 6:00 a.m. Sure. Right. We've seen this movie already. By 4:00 a.m. every mini-stalactite on the stucco ceiling is imprinted forever on our brains. By 5:00 a.m. we are standing in the driveway, packed bags at our sides, swatting at large, invisible flying creatures and peering into the inky blackness for the faintest glimmer of headlights.

The cab shows up precisely at 6:00. Which only makes us more nervous.

It carries us swiftly and deposits us at the passenger terminal in plenty of time. Now we know disaster looms.

Our flight takes off on schedule, flies flawlessly and lands with barely a poof of tires in Toronto. By now we're both sweating visibly. Customs is a breeze. Our car is — oh, diabolical! — right where we left it. We go home. We go to bed. We get up. And for two solid days we answer the obvious question. "How was your trip?" everyone asks.

And we always answer the same way. We say, "Well, we didn't get sick. . . ."

A Canuck in the D.R.

A CANADIAN EMBARKS ON a short, sharp midwinter Caribbean vacation with a certain amount of trepidation. Especially if that vacation is to unfold in the Dominican Republic. The D.R., as travel agents like to call it, is not after all, Myrtle Beach or Malibu. It is the eastern two-thirds of the second-largest island in the West Indies, with cloud-shrouded mountain ranges, lizard-green valleys, beaches so white that they hurt the eye, and a Spanish-speaking population still emerging from under the shadow of one of the most brutal dictators ever spawned in an area that grows them like, well, bananas.

Rafael Trujillo ran the Dominican Republic as his personal fiefdom, charnel house and brothel for thirty-one years, until he was thoughtfully blown away by his own military officers in 1961. One hates to say it, but Trujillo makes the case for assassination as a credible political solution. The man was a pig, as well as a thief and a murderer. Washington thought he was swell because he was also anti-Communist.

But that's in the past. Today the Dominion Republic, while not exactly a classical Athenian democracy, is definitely a better place to live for the average Dominican than it was under Trujillo. A big part of the reason for that is tourists. They leave several hundred million dollars on the island every year. The D.R. is keen on tourists. Canadian tourists particularly. Why Canucks? I'm not sure. Perhaps it's because Dominicans once maintained their own professional baseball team in Canada — the Blue Jays. Maybe it's because from a Dominican perspective Canadians are the ultimate tourists — polite, sun starved and rich. And we are rich. The D.R.

makes you very aware of that. Julio, our guide on a tour bus, is asked what the monthly wage is for a Dominican. It depends, he says, on whether you work for the government or for free enterprise. Government employees make a minimum of 400 pesos a month. Under free enterprise they must be paid at least 500 a month.

Several square miles of sugar cane plantation swim by the bus window as the Canadian passengers try to visualize living in Toronto or Trois-Rivières or Tuktoyaktuk on the equivalent of eighty to a hundred Canadian dollars a month.

And what about all that sugar cane out the window? It's virtually an ocean of green that stretches out sometimes from horizon to horizon. "Say, Hoolio, how do ya harvest all this sugar cane?" yells a ruddy-faced farm boy from Georgetown, Ontario. "You got binders? Combines?" "Machete," says Julio. Another large silence.

But the Dominicans are not a mournful lot. If they have been dealt a shabby hand in the economic poker game of twentieth-century global politics, they don't moon over it. They seem remarkably buoyant and unscarred by their lower standard of living. Perhaps it has something to do with living in a sun-splashed tropical paradise where the entire citizenry looks like Tahitian extras from *Mutiny on the Bounty*, manna grows on trees and there is no expression for the term "snow tires."

Not that my entire trip to the Dominican was what you'd call Eden in a hammock. There were long, tedious stretches of what I'd have to call the worst of Banana Republicanism . . . hours spent in crocodile lineups that went nowhere . . . chewing on cold, old, absurdly overpriced pseudofood . . . fretting over disappeared luggage . . . being ignored by surly, lazy natives . . .

Mind you . . . once I got out of Pearson International Airport, everything was fine.

Terrorism in Labrador

I WANT TO TAKE you away from where you are right now. I want you to imagine that you are camping in the wilderness. Hundreds of miles beyond horn honks and factory whistles. You are in front of a pup tent on the shores of a small lake in remote Labrador. Getting used to the real-life sounds. The ones that have been there for thousands of years. The call of the loon, the chirp of crickets. The splash of a jumping fish. The soughing of the wind through spruce boughs. You are . . . calming down. Peeling off layer after layer of protective urban calluses. You're getting gentle again . . . and then . . .

The air around you tears open like a burst zipper. Your ears are raped . . . by a sledgehammer of sound, louder than any sound you've ever heard, louder than any sound you can imagine. So loud you can't even tell that it *is* a sound. It's a . . . force so loud it's like being mugged inside your mind.

Then just as suddenly — it's gone. And you find yourself gasping, ten feet from where you were ten seconds ago, on your knees, hands clamped to the sides of your head.

What was that? Earthquake? Meteorite? Brain seizure?

None of the above. It was just a jet. A NATO jet. Happens all the time in Labrador. Well, not all the time. Say . . . nineteen, twenty times a day? Seven thousand flights a year. Canadian jets, German jets, British jets, Dutch jets. They fly out of Canadian Forces Base Goose Bay on what they call low-level training flights, skimming along the earth at treetop level at hundreds of miles an hour.

Know how loud that is for any living creature they happen to fly over? Imagine having your head lashed to one of those megaspeakers at a Who rock concert so that your ear is mashed against the mesh. Now imagine the Who playing Pinball Wizard at full amplification.

That's not loud enough.

Rock music peaks at 110, 115 decibels. A jet plane passing a hundred feet away is more than 140 decibels. Twenty decibels above the pain threshold. Loud enough to cause permanent ear damage.

So it's a good job these flights take place over Labrador where nobody lives, right? Wrong. Nearly 10,000 people live there. Innu. They are not a violent people. They're kind of shy, as a matter of fact. But these flights are driving them to distraction. Their argument is pretty straightforward. They point out that they have lived in the area for at least nine millennia — which is about 8,950 years longer than the military base. It's their land, they say. And the NATO jets are ruining their hunting, their peace of mind, their lives.

Our Defence department maintains that the pilots make every effort not to fly over native camps, caribou migration routes or calving grounds, but the Brass doesn't have a lot of time to play nursemaid to restless natives. It's too busy lobbying to have Goose Bay chosen as the new expanded NATO weapons flight-training centre. If that goes through, the number of low-level flights over Labrador would increase from 7,000 to 40,000 a year. That works out to about 110 flights a day, seven days a week.

So far the Innu's pleas to stop the deafening flights have . . . fallen on deaf ears.

A pity the Innu don't have a small air force of their own. One Voodoo jet just skimming Parliament Hill at 800 miles an hour might do wonders for their case. Might even wake up the folks inside.

The Fallen Arches of Civilization

I am inclined to notice the ruin in things, perhaps because I was born in Italy.

ARTHUR MILLER

WELL, MY LAST NAME isn't Miller and I never got to snuggle up to Marilyn Monroe, but aside from that, the playwright and I are practically identical twins on the subject of ruins. I love 'em, too — probably because I was born in Toronto, where old buildings are considered pornographic, something to be torn down and rendered into parking lots as quickly as possible. I don't think I got to see a proper ruin until I was about twenty-five and went hitchhiking across Europe. Never could keep my mouth quite closed at places like Stonehenge and Cordoba and the Roman Colosseum.

Heck, I don't have to go *that* far back. I could sit in a seedy old pub in some one-lorry town in the English countryside playing the rubbernecked colonial as I drank in the sagging roofbeams, the crazily canted floorboards, the ancient bric-a-brac on the walls that may not have been dusted since Cromwell's time.

It was a thrill to realize that Sam Pepys, Chris Marlowe, even Bill Shakespeare himself might have sat on that selfsame stool, staring into a similar overpriced pint of warm draught ale.

It was never very hard to tell the locals from the tourists — the locals always ignored the relics that surrounded them.

I remember passing through a tiny hamlet in Kent and spying the strangest tower I have ever seen.

I think it was a tower. It stood, or rather leaned, on a bare patch of ground right in the centre of the hamlet. Architecturally it looked like a very young child's first experiment with clay, except that it was about twenty feet tall and obviously very old — there was moss growing up one side of it, and here and there the butt ends of rotting timbers poked through its flanks. What made the tower totally incongruous was the door at the base of it. It was a perfectly fashioned wooden door with a wooden jamb — except that it was no more than three feet high. An adult would have to get down on his hands and knees to enter.

I stood and looked at that tower for as long as I could bear it, then I did what any dopey, gawking tourist would do — I went into the nearest pub, ordered a pint of bitter and in my best, uninterested tone asked the barkeep what the tower outside was all about.

"Wot tower would that be, sorr?"

And this I swear is true: I had to take the bartender to the window and point out the erection that loomed not thirty feet from his door.

"Oh, *that*," he murmured, massaging a wattled jaw, "I don't really know, sorr . . . it were always there . . ."

I suppose you could become that blasé, growing up in a land choc-a-bloc with antiquities — maybe it's a healthier attitude than the undue enthusiasm we North Americans exhibit towards what some wag called "civilization's fallen arches."

It may very well be that in our zeal, some ruins are being "loved to death." The famous prehistoric cave paintings at Lascaux, France, have been closed to the public — carbon dioxide from tourists' breath was causing the pigment to fade and disappear.

Similarly, tourist traffic at Stonehenge in England has become so intense that a couple of years ago there was talk of hanging up a Closed sign and erecting a duplicate site nearby.

It would look exactly like Stonehenge except the slabs of rock would be made of plastic.

Fortunately, cooler heads prevailed, but I wonder if it would have worked? I wonder if tourists would have flocked to photograph a polyurethane Clonehenge? After all, we flock by the millions to Disney World and Canada's Wonderland, and what are they but mountains and jungles and castles of plastic?

And then there's that recent bulletin from federal historians in Ontario — the one asking Canadians to send in any old photographs they might have of the ruins at the country estate of former prime minister William Lyon Mackenize King.

You may remember that at great expense the slightly dotty King imported the remains of European turrets and battlements, then scattered the rubble around his Kingsmere estate outside Ottawa in an effort to make the place seem more Old Worldish.

Problem is, those ruins are getting . . . well, ruined. The original crumbling arches and mouldering walls are crumbling and mouldering beyond recognition, and the historians hope they can work from old photographs to restore them to their original, er, um, ruinous condition.

Well, it may seem wacky to you and me, but I'm sure Mackenzie King would understand.

Christopher Who?

I HAVE NO IDEA when the next earthquake will shiver San Francisco's timbers, but I can predict with absolute certainty when the next big North American flood will come.

It's on the doorstep, folks. Watch for it in 1992.

What are they going to call this flood? I'm not sure. Christofrenzy, maybe. Or Columbomania. Whatever they call it, it will definitely strike our shores in 1992. Why? Because 1992 is exactly 500 years later than 1492, that's why. Which makes it the five-hundredth anniversary of Columbus's discovery of North America.

And there will be celebrations. You will see a rash of books, a spate of TV specials, a clutch of Hollywood movies.

And an absolute mint of coins and medals.

Christopher Columbus has been one of the favourite subjects for the folks who turn out coins, tokens and medals. Depictions of the famous Italian and/or his equally famous ships, the *Nina*, the *Pinta* and the *Santa Maria*, have appeared on coins from Spain, Portugal, Denmark, Costa Rica, Brazil and Iceland as well as Canada and the United States.

Which is not surprising. Discovery of the New World and proving that the world was not flat were two crucial developments that changed terrestrial history.

There's just one tiny problem.

Colombus doesn't deserve the credit for either discovery. He was a Christopher-come-lately on both counts.

Knowledge that the earth was round, not flat? Earthlings with a shred of scientific knowledge had known that for centuries before

Columbus presented his credentials to Queen Isabella in the Spanish court. The Romans portrayed the earth as a globe in the year 20 A.D. An Arab scientist by the name of Al Maqdisi had figured out that the Earth had 360 degrees of longitude and 180 degrees of latitude in the tenth century — nearly five hundred years before Columbus waddled up the gangplank of the *Santa Maria.*

And another thing our high school history books failed to make clear — Columbus was no noble explorer in pursuit of pure knowledge. His four voyages were business trips, pure and simple. The expeditions were bankrolled by Spaniards, including Queen Isabella, on the express understanding that Columbus would bring back plunder — gold, jewels, spices — whatever he and his cutthroats could lay their hands on.

Columbus accepted the gamble because, after all, he thought he was taking a short cut to Asia, where booty was easy to come by. You can imagine his surprise when he fetched up instead on the palm-fringed shores of the island of San Salvador. No cities. No gold statues. Not a jewellery store in sight.

Columbus panicked. He owed big bucks to his sponsors back in Madrid, and they weren't the forgiving kind. Frantically, he raced from one Caribbean island to the next, stealing anything he could get his hands on.

Which wasn't much. There were, after all, no great civilizations in the Caribbean islands in the fifteenth century. Just a bunch of peaceful Indian tribes who greeted the visitors with wide-eyed wonder. The Taino Indians on the island of Hispaniola were particularly hospitable. Columbus paid them back by seizing 1,200 of them, throwing them in his ships' holds and shipping them back to Spain. The ones who survived the trip were paraded through the streets of Seville naked, then sold as slaves.

Not to put too fine a point on it, Columbus was no humanitarian. He was also not the discoverer of the New World. Vikings were in Newfoundland in the eleventh century. Some historians believe that St. Brendan the Navigator touched these shores in 565 A.D. The supreme irony is that Columbus, famous in our history books for discovering America, never even set foot on our continent.

Well, maybe not the supreme irony. That honour goes to a friend of mine, Pat Ningwance. I said to her, "Pat, do you realize that Columbus didn't discover North America at all? Isn't that shocking?" Pat just looked at me for a long time. Saying nothing.

Then I remembered. Pat's an Ojibway.

California: The Scribbler's Friend

HERE ARE THREE reasons I wouldn't trade newspaper column writing for any other listing in the Yellow Pages.

(a) no dress code

(b) great working hours (anytime you want)

(c) no Christmas office party

Here is one reason I sometimes dream of giving up this line of work in favour of dew-worm picking, wolverine wrestling or operating a ham-sandwich franchise in Jerusalem:

(a) you have to do it

Every

Week.

Toothache? Too bad. Wife left you? Tough. Transmission on the station wagon sounds as if it's having baby transmissions without benefit of anesthetic? Message on your answering machine urging you to call Revenue Canada by yesterday at latest? That little flutter under your left nipple seems to be coming back more often and staying longer?

Yon editor with the mustard-seed-size heart still wants his 1,500 words and couldja make it a little more *up*beat, fer cryin' out loud?

But that's not the worst of it. The worst of column writing rolls around every year right after Canada Day. The Dog Days of summer, when the entire world seems to take the phone off the hook and go on vacation. School's out. Parliament, that virtual shooting gallery of column topics, has a Closed for the Season sign hanging on the door, and the rest of the world seems to have gone to the cottage. Nothing is happening. Ergo, there's nothing to write about.

Well, almost nothing. There is one failsafe, general-interest topic that any columnist can turn to when all the other columnial water-holes have dried up.

It's called California. Its nickname is the Golden State but that should be changed to the Breakfast Cereal State, because there are more nuts and flakes per square inch of California turf than you'll find this side of a Three Stooges Retrospective.

Want me to prove it? Okay. Exhibit A: this recent issue of the *Los Angeles Times*. Page one carries a nice graduation story datelined Fresno. It's about a petite eighteen-year-old named Joely Kragh. There's a photo of Joely — five foot two, eighty-six pounds — demurely holding up the present her folks got her for making it through high school.

It's a snub-nosed .38 caliber revolver. She's taking it with her to the University of California this fall. "I have read a lot of articles about rape and murder, and the prospect of being alone at night without any means of defense worried me," said Joely.

The largest city in California is Los Angeles — largest city in the world perhaps, if you take your measurements in pavement. L.A. is the town where cops will stop and ask you what you're up to if they find you walking on the street. Nobody walks in L.A. Nobody takes public transit, either. They can't find it. Oh well, there's always the famous expressways — if you don't mind people taking pot shots at you. You heard about the Expressway Murders? A small article here on page three of my copy of the *Los Angeles Times* says the two best-selling bumper stickers right now read "Don't shoot — I'm reloading" and "Cover me — I'm changing lanes."

Ah, but here's the story I've been waiting for — tucked into the bottom left-hand corner of page eight. Vintage California. It's datelined Santa Ana and it tells how Robert Hanshew has been fined $58 for illegally using the expressway car pool lane. L.A. law stipulates that during rush hour, cars in the fast lane must contain at least two people. Bob Hanshew was stopped last month by the LAPD. "S'amatter?" groused Hanshew, jerking his thumb at the two figures in his back seat. "I got two passengers."

"Yes," the police officer agreed, "but they're dead, sir."

Frozen, in fact. Bob Hanshew works as a driver for a mortuary service. The judge ruled that cadavers don't qualify as car pool members.

Nice try, Bob, but I guess you have to be alive to qualify for life in the fast lane.

Even in California.

PART 5
The Stuff We Collect

Ahoy, There —
It's for You

WHAT DO YOU SAY after your phone goes *brrrinnnnnngggggg* and you pick it up?

You say hello, right? Most of us do. Oh, I know some no-nonsense business types who say "Joe Blow here" or "Mary Jane speaking." I even knew one laconic bartender who used to hook the receiver under his chin and drawl, "Your dime, my time," as he worked the draft-beer pump.

Well, I just thought you ought to know that but for a simple twist of fate we might all be picking up the phone and hollering, "Ahoy! Ahoy!" each time it rings.

That's how George Willard Cay wanted it to be. George was a telephone pioneer — North American's first full-time telephone operator, as a matter of fact. He worked one of the very early primitive switchboards for the District Telephone Company of New Haven, Connecticut, 'way back in 1889. Everybody who placed a call had to go through George and every time George fielded an incoming call he greeted the caller with a shouted, "Ahoy! Ahoy!"

But despite Cay's indefatigable efforts to educate the public, the jaunty nautical expression never quite caught on as a telephone greeting. We chose the blandly neutral hello instead.

Pity. If we'd followed in Cay's wake, telephone etiquette might have picked up a colourful sea-going tinge.

Wouldn't it be satisfying to call up some sleazy bill collector who'd been hounding you and open with "Avast, ye barnacle-scabbed scow master! Call off your boarding parties or I'll let fly a broadside that'll take the wind out of your sails!"

If we'd listened to Cay we could all sound like salty old sea dogs when the phone rings.

Speaking of which — ever thought about why it does? Ring, I mean? Ever wonder why a telephone doesn't buzz or honk or blatt or squeak or grunt?

My theory is quite simple. The telephone doesn't honk because the name of the man who invented it was not Alexander Graham Honk.

It was Bell. A. G. Bell. And bells, as any school kid knows, ring.

Actually, that's a tradition we're losing, too, isn't it? Telephones don't ring anymore. Not in my office, anyway.

I don't know quite how to describe the unpleasant electronic whinneying sound my office telephone makes now, except to say that it sounds like an adding machine in the final stages of a difficult labour.

That's not the only big change in Dr. Bell's infernal little gizmo, of late. Telephones are mating like minks and showing up in the damnedest places. Used to be there was a telephone in the front hall and maybe a phone booth down by the Texaco station, and that was about it. But not anymore. Nowadays any self-respecting yuppie household boasts a telephone in the bathroom, the bedroom, the kitchen, the parlour and out by the pool.

The latest rage for anybody who has a thousand bucks they don't know what to do with? Why, the cellular phone, of course. Fits right in your car so that you can take calls offering you magazine subscriptions and free broadloom estimates as you drive down the parkway.

It will be a rainy day at Hades Central Switchboard before this phoneophobe installs one of these instruments of torture in his car. Heck, the only good thing I know about driving these days is that there's always a chance of finding a nice cosy traffic jam where nobody can reach me on the phone.

You don't drive a car? You still can't escape. We have "floater" phones. Portable wedges of molded plastic that can hook onto your belt just in case you were thinking of fleeing to the garden to get away with from your worldly cares.

Personally, I'm holding out for the next big telecommunications breakthrough.

The phoneless cord.

Water on the Wrist

Pssssst. LOOKING FOR something special for that Ms. Picky or Mr. Finicky on your Christmas list? Boy, did you come to the right place — got just the number for you. It's a wrist watch. Battery operated, digital readout with one little extra. This watch won't work unless it's wet. That's right — wet. Doesn't have to be wet *all* all the time, you understand. You don't have to walk around carrying your watch in a bag of water like a goldfish from Woolworth's. But unless you wear it in the shower, drive through a car wash with your wrist out the window, or drag your arm through a mud puddle at least once every couple of weeks, this watch won't work.

Devereux Limited, the company that produces this watch in a variety of, one presumes, waterproof colours, says their new product will be the latest fad to sweep the nation, starting any day now. Soon as the watch catches on, Devereux has a new line of water calculators and water clock radios waiting thirstily in the wings.

I hear you. Why, you are wondering, would anyone want to buy a wrist watch that requires its own water bowl? You're a cynic. You're the kind of person who would scoff at the importance of having gorilla-proof luggage or pickup trucks that can scale mountains of rubble. I'll bet you're the kind of person who sneered at those great old Timex television commercials where they strapped watches to outboard motor propellors, threw them off cliffs and dropped them into working cement mixers, only to retrieve them hours later still triumphantly ticking. Why, I'll bet if I looked at your wrist right now I'd discover you're wearing a watch that not only doesn't give the time in Shanghai or the humidity in Brasilia but isn't even waterproof to a depth of 315 feet.

Thought so.

You know what causes that? An old childhood trauma. Your subconscious probably remembers getting cuffed on the earhole as a kid for *getting* your watch wet . . . and you can't break out of that old fear.

Well, *you* can wallow in ancient guilt trips, if you want. I think Devereux Limited and their water-powered wrist watch represent the wave of the future. It's time to reconfigure our antiquated thought patterns and look at old products in a new light.

Me, I'm off to corner the Canadian market in pencils. I plan to remarket them as portable cordless word processors with infinite megabyte capacity. The deluxe models will come with a unitized lightweight data-bank obliterator — that'll take care of the ones with erasers.

And if that takes off this Christmas season (as I'm sure it will), my next commercial coup should cut the ground right out from under Devereux Limited and their water watch. I intend to offer a solar-powered analogue day timer with a plus-minus accuracy rating of a fraction of a nanosecond. This beauty will be constructed entirely of non-toxic organic components. It'll be waterproof, shockproof and utterly impervious to dust, magnetism or power brownouts. My only design problem is coming up with a strap strong enough to hold this to your wrist. It's a stone disk about the size of a coffee table with a bronze thingee in the middle.

The Greeks called them sundials — but what did they know about marketing?

Inventions We Could Live Without

T HE CHINESE, INSCRUTABLE rascals that they are, have a great
saying: "May you live in interesting times." When they say it
to you, they do it stonefaced so you can't tell whether it's a blessing
or a curse they're laying on you.

We live in interesting times. Maybe *the* most interesting times
this tired old planet's ever hosted, if "interesting" is synonymous
with variety and profusion and rapid change. Lotta change. My
grandfather never saw an airplane in flight. My grandson is liable
to end up flying off for a round of golf on Mars.

And inventions. Someone figured out that there have been
more scientific inventions in the past twenty years than in all
previous human history put together.

Which brings me to my modest proposal. I would like them to
stop. Inventing things, I mean. More than that. I would appreciate
if they would recall three or four recent breakthroughs.

PIP, for instance. PIP is the name of a new line of television
sets — PIP standing for Picture in a Picture. Which is what you
get: two different pictures on your television screen simultaneously. "You can watch two hockey games at the same time,"
burbles the PIP brochure. No, thanks. One is confusing enough.
Besides, I know what would be on my screen most of the time.
Not simultaneous games . . . simultaneous beer commercials. PIP,
may you RIP.

The Japanese have come up with an invention in a similar vein.
It's a telephone that projects a black-and-white picture of the
person you have on the line. This is not a television screen. The
picture is just a still photograph.

144

Is this truly a step forward? I would find it a trifle unreal to be, say, shouting death threats at my agent over the phone, while looking at an eight-by-ten glossy of him grinning back at me. And I can have this thrill, you tell me, for a mere $400? Sorry Japan, wrong number.

Here's another Japanese brainwave that's going to do for the collective nose what Muzak has done for the collective ear. It's a system that circulates selected odours through the ventilating ducts of large buildings. There's even a smell menu to choose from. Want to put your customers in a happy buying mood? Pump in a little Cyprus Grove aroma. That'll get the charge cards rattling. They recommend a lavender scent for offices and a snappy peppermint smell for conference rooms. Well, I must admit the possible applications are intriguing. A piped-in smell of bacon and eggs would probably lever me out of bed in the morning. Pulp mills could spray a little Arrid Extra Dry or Brut into their stacks to disguise their stench. And for the House of Commons we could pump in — naw, let's step around that.

Which brings me to my last dubious invention. Nabisco Brands Inc. is now selling breath mints. For dogs.

Well, as owner of a dog whose breath has been known to blanch dark furniture and send houseguests reeling on their backs, I can't say it's a totally bad idea, but it seems unsportsman-like, somehow. Surreptitious breath mints. Involuntary odor suppression. Isn't there something in the Geneva Convention about that?

In any case, you can be sure Nabisco didn't ask the dogs what they thought about it, but then again, maybe they were afraid to take a poll. As John Diefenbaker said, you know what dogs do to polls.

The Death Business

I'M GLAD PERRIN BEATTY isn't our Minister of Defence anymore. Not because he's incompetent or anything. *Au contraire*. Mr. Beatty is a highly gifted, extremely able politician — quite possibly the sturdiest mushroom ever to bloom on the Tory compost heap.

No, what disqualifies Mr. Beatty for the Defence portfolio is that one chilling physical deformity that stares back at you from every photograph ever taken of the man.

He's too good-looking for the job.

Baby-faced, actually. Anyone whose job description calls for him to play with guns and hobnob with war hawks should appear a tad . . . gritty. A Defence minister ought to look pugnacious like Charles Bronson, or vulpine like Caspar Weinberger, or hugely menacing like hedgehog-browed Brezhnev.

Hockey player Tiger Williams, with his scars and lumps and his deadpan "you wanna settle this out in the alley" stare — that's the kind of look a Defence minister needs.

The thought of the cherubic Perrin Beatty juggling MX missiles and troop displacements and lobbing nuclear submarines into our Arctic, all with that angelic, choirboy smile on his face, seemed vaguely obscene to me.

Kind of like dressing Bambi in jungle fatigues.

But then it's an obscene business, the war game. Maybe that's what made the beatific Mr. Beatty's participation so jarring. I had the same experience this morning, leafing through a magazine called *Armed Forces Journal International*. It's an American publication designed to keep us up to date on the latest in bombs,

146

rockets, warplanes, land mines and other flesh-shredding technology.

There's an ad in there from a company called BEI Defense Systems Co. extolling the virtues of a rocket that can knock enemy aircraft right out of the sky. The ad shows a panoramic wilderness scene of craggy mountains that could be the Canadian Rockies, with a clutch of Tom Thomson-ish jack pines silhouetted against the setting sun.

That's the peaceful part of the ad. Above the landscape you can see a big assault helicopter all decked out in camouflage paint. It is in the process of being blown into tiny pieces of scrap by a BEI Defense Systems Co. rocket.

But here's the special feature of this glossy full-page advertisement: the whole illustration is covered with tiny plastic bubbles. Break one with your thumbnail and — zowie! — yes, the actual smell of gunpowder.

Great Moments in Advertising: Scratch 'n' Sniff brings you the smell of imminent violent death.

Typical American wretched excess, you say? Don't feel too smug. A few years ago, Ottawa hosted a cosy little garage sale called ARMX '89. Actually, there was nothing little about it. ARMX '89 was a huge international weapons show. Gun runners, Banana Republic generals, military "advisers" and other assorted merchants of death convened on the banks of the Rideau to kick the treads on the latest in military assault vehicles and discuss kill ratios with the helpful, courteous staff. Two hundred of the exhibiting firms were Canadian.

And how did our own government feel about having a war bazaar nestled in its bosom? Delighted, thank you very much. The Feds may have lacked the gonads to speak up for simple human decency in the Salman Rushdie affair, but if it's guns and bombs you want to flog, the welcome mat is always out.

Does that sound bitter? Well, yeah, I am. I've got two kids. I don't care for the thought of half-witted hawks strutting around with nukes on their hips, dicing with the future of the planet.

But don't take a middle-aged peacenik's word for it. Listen to an expert:

"Every gun that is made, every warship launched, every rocket fired signifies in a final sense, a theft from those who hunger and

147

are not fed, from those who are cold and not clothed. This 'world in arms' is not spending money alone: it is spending the sweat of its labourers, the genius of its scientists and the hopes of its children."

I didn't say that. A general did.

Fellow by the name of Dwight D. Eisenhower.

Man's Worst Invention — Bra None

WELL, THE BIG NEWS this week is that we are all sitting poised on the cusp — or perhaps that's "cups" — of the world's brassiere centennial.

Yes, according to Undergarment Mythology, it was one hundred years ago that a Parisian shopkeeper took a pair of tin snips and sheared off the bottom 90 per cent of a whalebone corset, leaving just the upper double-barrelled slingshot and an opportunity for women of fashion to take their first deep breath since puberty.

Maybe the bra was invented in France a hundred years ago. Patriotic Americans clutch Mary Phelps Jacobs to *their* bosom. They say Mary whipped two handkerchiefs, some pink ribbon and a hank of thread together and came up with what she called "the backless brassiere" twenty-five years later.

So the brassiere is either a hundred years old or seventy-five years old. My question is: why are we celebrating?

Is there any other single accoutrement, not excluding the Rack and the Iron Maiden, which has been the agent of more pain, suffering and humiliation — not to mention misinformation — than the bra? I grew up in an era when all female breasts were buttressed by angora sweaters draped over what appeared to be, in silhouette, two oil funnels on a strap. I took it as a given that naked female breasts looked like the isoceles triangles in my geometry text. I could only assume that the unencumbered native maidens who graced the pages of *National Geographic* were some kind of genetically defective hybrids found only in foreign lands.

When I finally got a chance to see for myself the true proportions and parameters of de-bra-ed feminine pulchritude, I kind of destroyed the romantic potential of the moment by rearing back and screaming, "Medic!"

I was fairly rattled by that point, anyway, having fumbled myself witless with that feature of the bra that makes it the least loved piece of apparel on the planet — the Gordian knot that welds the damn thing together. Who invented the bra hook, anyway? Rubik, I suspect.

Mind you, Howard Hughes had a worse case of Bra Blues than I ever did. He worked up four pages of engineering notes, trying to design a cantilevered Cross Your Heart that would contain Jane Russell's twin defiances of gravity. We all know how Howard Hughes ended up.

It's just as well, too. Howard couldn't have handled the bra scene of today. We've got push-up bras, training bras, padded bras, nursing bras, wired bras, jogging bras, soft bras, and no bras at all. We even have, thanks to Madonna and her ilk, fashion bras — bras you wear on top of your clothing.

Meanwhile, on the other side of the gender fence, I am looking right now at a newspaper photograph of a guy — yes, a guy — wearing the Empathy Belly. The Empathy Belly is a new product that looks kind of like a baseball umpire's chest protector on growth hormones. It has two droopy padded breasts and a basketball-size belly. The belly contains a pendulum and metal balls to simulate prenatal kicking. The Empathy Belly is designed to help guys know what it feels like to be eight and nine-tenths months pregnant. It looks an awful lot like the whalebone corsets that bras replaced a hundred years ago.

So that's where we stand after one century of the brassiere. Women wearing them over their clothes, if they wear them at all. Men gravitating towards the Empathy Belly. We've come a long way, uhhh . . . buddy.

And if angora sweaters make a comeback, I don't want to hear about it.

Let's Get Purse-onal

I DON'T KNOW Mr. Taj Kassam of Edmonton from Mr. Adam of Eden, but we share a vision, Taj and I.

We both see a future full of purse-carrying men.

Mind you, Mr. Kassam has a vested interest in the vision — he's owner of an Edmonton store called The Leather Place. One of his main product lines is a small leather carry-all with a shoulder strap designed to do the job of a wallet and pockets, and it's suitable for either sex. It's a purse, but Mr. Kassam doesn't call it that because most men would not feel comfortable walking into a store and saying, "I'd like to buy a purse, please." Men would never buy perfume for themselves, either — but they line up to buy "men's fragrances" by the barrel. Ditto with the "man's purse" concept. Solution: don't call it a purse; call it a "unisex bag."

Mr. Kassam admits that so far the male demand for his unisex bags in the macho burg of Edmonton has been distinctly underwhelming, but he wasn't expecting doorcrashers, anyway. "In Alberta, you don't see men carrying them around much," he says. "It's a real no-no here."

But Taj Kassam has the patience of a philosopher. He's willing to wait because he thinks the tide is about to turn.

What's going to make men more amenable to the idea of carrying a pu — all right, a unisex bag? Simple, according to Mr. Kassam.

The Loonie.

Taj Kassam thinks the brassy, eleven-sided dollar coins are eventually going to convince men that carrying a bag is a reasonable idea.

He has a point. Good old greenbacks have been sucked out of circulation all over Canada. Every dollar bill that returned to

Ottawa was snagged, shredded and replaced by a Loonie. Nowadays, the change that comes back from just about anything you purchase inevitably includes one- or two-dollar coins.

So now men have very lumpy pockets.

Well, you can see Taj Kassam's theory, can't you? He figures men won't want to walk around with their pants pockets looking like squirrel cheeks. They're going to cast around for some fashionable new method of toting about their disposable income.

Taj Kassam hopes they're walking by his store at that moment so he can sell them a unisex bag. "It won't be dramatic, it'll be gradual," he says. And he thinks it'll start with your executives between twenty-five and thirty. "They're more adapted to change than other age groups."

Well, true-confession time, folks. I'm no young executive and I'm on the far side of thirty, but I've been carrying a bag for years. I carry it because I don't like sitting on my wallet, patting pockets for my car keys or jingling when I walk. I also like to carry things like notebooks, sketch pads and novels that I haven't quite finished reading.

Do I ever get razzed about carrying a bag? Nah. I've got a beard, broad shoulders and I weigh about 200 pounds. I don't look exactly limp of wrist. Besides, let me give you an inventory of what I'm carrying in my bag right now:

a ring full of keys
a calendar/date book
a pen knife
a "lucky" rock (approximate weight eight ounces)
three ball-point pens
a couple of months' worth of gas receipts
one Elmore Leonard murder mystery
sunglasses
a wallet

You don't want to razz me. If I hit you with my purse you might never get off the floor.

Taj Kassam thinks Loonies will make other men take up shoulder bags, but that creates another problem for me. I don't have room for Loonies. My bag's full. I think the Loonie deluge is going to bunt me towards my next fashion accessory: a monogrammed shopping cart.

Some of us are simply destined to be slightly ahead of our time.

Earl's Dead

THIS IS A THREE-MINUTE essay on why I think Earl the Cat might be funny. Earl the Cat, for anyone who's been at the cottage, watching "King of Kensington" reruns or otherwise out of touch for the past couple of weeks, is a pussy of the species *felinus defunctus*. Earl's a thoroughly dead cat. He just lies there, kind of flat looking, his four legs and his tail splayed out like the limbs of an iron-deficient starfish. Earl's dead, all right . . . but don't break out the black crêpe and the organ music just yet. Earl is made of plush and stuffing. He's got a little tag on his bum telling you that he contains certain man-made fibres and should not be machine washed. Earl's a toy. Like a Teddy Bear. Earl the Dead Cat is a joke.

Pretty good one, too, when you think about it — I mean, from a commercial point of view. How many people can you count up that (a) hate cats, (b) love cats but because of space, lifestyle or a resident pit bull, can't *have* cats or (c) are between cats?

Doncha see? Earl the Cat's a perfect pet for folks like that. He's cute and cuddly, but he doesn't shed, doesn't meow for a can of Miss Mew Gourmet Surprise, doesn't lacerate the chesterfield or leave odiferous calling cards in inaccessible places, doesn't bring mice to your door, amorous toms to your window or fleas to your ankle — Earl the Cat doesn't do any of those things. Earl can't. He's dead.

Now I'll go out on a limb here and say that I think the person who invented Earl the Cat is some kind of minor marketing genius. But the Ontario Humane Society would not agree. Reading between the lines of a press release issued by the society recently, I would guess that they rank the inventor of Earl the Cat somewhere between Cujo and Ivan the Terrible. The Society press release says the public should boycott Earl the Cat, because the message Earl delivers to children is that a cat's life is worthless.

Oh, well now, I don't know about all that. I figure I must have watched about eleven million Tom and Jerry cartoons since I was a kid. I've seen poor Tom get blown up, shot down, run over by steam rollers and chewed on by bulldogs. I've seen him shotgunned, dynamited, electrocuted and dropped from high buildings without benefit of safety net. Has all this made me callous and unfeeling towards cats — specifically towards the resident furred monarch who condescends to take bed and board at my house? Would I ever think of treating my cat, Lassie, with anything less than the absolute regal deference he has always taken as his due?

Are you kidding? He'd swat me silly in a second.

Lassie would probably agree with the Ontario SPCA — he wouldn't think Earl the Cat is very funny. But then he doesn't think anything is funny. He doesn't have to. He's a cat.

Me . . . I have to say I do think Earl's funny — and I'm not worried that he sets a bad example for Canada's youth. I think kids can distinguish between illusion and reality — even if some adults have trouble. Besides, if the SPCA is truly concerned about Earl the Dead Cat's subliminal message, I have distressing news for them.

You know all Earl's companions on the toy shelves — the Teddy Bears, the Barbie and the Cabbage Patch and the Mickey Mouse and Garfield dolls?

Well, don't let it get around, but . . . *they're dead, too!*

The Tissue Issue

NO TIME. THAT'S WHAT'S wrong with this fast-forward, overdrive world we live in. No time to sit back and contemplate the simple, blessed things that make a joy of everyday life. Things like sunrises. Long weekends. And . . . well, toilet paper.

Yes, toilet paper. I realize it is neither customary nor chic to sing the praises of that yeoman cylinder on the bathroom wall, but sing them I plan to. Let other scribblers wax rhapsodic about daffodils, Grecian urns and manic depressive Danish princelings, I want to take a shot at immortalizing three-ply Delsey.

Actually the very fact that I can mention toilet paper in a book is evidence of impressive progress for this furled friend of mankind.

One hundred and fifty years ago, the editor (yes, it was the same one) would have thought I was mad. Back in Victorian times one didn't speak of such vulgar things, much less write about them. Ladies and other gentle folk would murmur to their storekeeper of their need for "curl papers" for their hair, or "wrapping paper" for parcels. The storekeeper, every inch a hypocrite, would see to it that what they really wanted was discreetly tucked in the bottom of their shopping bags.

We didn't even have toilet paper as such until 1857 when an Englishman by the name of Joseph C. Gayetty gave the world "Gayetty's Medicated Paper . . . unbleached pearl-coloured pure Manila hemp paper, a perfectly pure article for the toilet and the prevention of piles." Still no roll, though. Gayetty came in packages of 500 sheets. Must have been pretty good stuff — old Joe charged fifty cents a package for it.

Unfortunately, not all toilet paper is — good stuff, I mean. In fact, when you consider that we've had 130-odd years to get the bugs out of Joe Gayetty's invention, it's amazing just how crummy some "bathroom tissue" is.

We're not too badly served in Canada. It's when you travel abroad that you begin to appreciate just how, ahem, rough the toilet paper situation can get. Public *servicios* in Spain serve up a spongy, crêpe-papery confection that tends to streeeeeeeeetch rather than tear. Many European public washrooms include a bored commissionaire with a saucer full of coins who asks you how many squares of paper you want.

The choices are: one or two. And a tip is expected.

I've heard horror stories about toilet paper in China, the Philippines and Mozambique; I've thrilled to whispered tales of deprivation and terror from travellers limping back from Macedonia and Novosibirsk; but the very worst toilet paper I ever personally encountered was in a "loo" in downtown London, England.

It wasn't on a cardboard roll. This stuff came in stiff sheets that sat in a tin dispenser riveted to the lavatory wall. Actually it couldn't have come on a roll. That would have required pliability and this stuff was about as flexible as a roof shingle. I don't think these so-called "tissues" had ever seen a pulp-and-paper mill; I think some lumberjack with a good eye and a keen axe just whacked them off the side of large trees in chips and sold them in stacks to the London Municipal Authority "as is."

You could see, I swear, actual slivers embedded in each sheet.

The most hilarious toilet paper I've ever seen came from London, too — from the British Museum, in fact, where bathroom tissue is provided in interfolded squares like Kleenex (only much, much flintier). Each sheet bears two legends. At the top it says "Property of Her Majesty's Government."

And at the bottom of each sheet the quintessentially prissy British admonition: "Now please wash your hands."

But good, bad or indifferent, at least we have toilet paper now. What did folks do before Joseph Gayetty, bless his inventive heart, papered his way to eternal glory?

Well, I can't speak for the entire human race, but I can pass along a little advice Lord Chesterfield wrote to his son, away back in 1747.

"I knew a gentleman," wrote milud, "who was so good a manager of his time that he would not even lose that small portion of it which the call of nature obliged him to pass in the necessary-house; but gradually went through all the Latin poets in those moments. He bought, for example, a common edition of Horace, of which he tore off gradually a couple of pages, carried them with him to that necessary place, read them first and then sent them down as a sacrifice to Cloacina; thus was so much time fairly gained; and I recommend you to follow his example."

Which brings me finally, to my all-time favourite toilet-paper story. It concerns Max Reger, a turn-of-the-century German composer who also did some reading in the "necessary-house" — even if he didn't always like what he read there. There was, for example, the time he read a negative review of one of his performances. A couple of days later the music critic responsible received a terse, three-sentence letter from Reger. It read:

"I am sitting in the smallest room of the house. I have your review in front of me. Soon it will be behind me."

And that, I trust, will serve as the absolute bottom line on toilet paper.

Smokeless Smokes

W HAT WOULD YOU DO if I gave you $325 million to spend? Not a bad assignment, eh? Let's see, $325 million would get you 1,300 Rolls-Royce Corniche convertibles. Three hundred and twenty-five million would probably pay for the conning tower on one of Canada's once-proposed Arctic nuclear submarines — heck, with that kind of dough you could probably still get a two-bedroom brick house in some parts of downtown Toronto.

The R. J. Reynolds Tobacco Company had $325 million burning a hole in its corporate pocket recently. The R. J. Reynolds people spent it on cigarettes.

Well, a cigarette, actually. A brand-new product. It is called Premier . . . the smokeless cigarette.

Now you and I might think that a smokeless cigarette sounds a little bit like a meatless steak or a kissless date, and we might be right.

But the tobacco folks are a little punch-drunk these days. They've seen ads for their product banned from magazines. They've seen tobacco use forbidden in planes, buses and restaurants. They've heard the highest official in American medicine, U.S. Surgeon General Everett Koop, condemn tobacco as the single biggest health hazard of the twentieth century.

So the folks who make cigarettes are desperate. Desperate enough to spend $325 million on the smokeless cigarette, a product that sounds as if it would have all the charisma of warm beer in a dog dish.

What kind of a cigarette do you get for that kind of money? Well, you get Premier. It's not like ordinary cigarettes — a wad of tobacco leaves packed into a cylinder of paper. The tip of a Premier cigarette contains a little charcoal puck. Behind the puck is an eensy-weensy aluminum capsule about the size of an aspirin. Inside the capsule are tiny beads containing dried tobacco, glycerin, and — just like your favourite breakfast cereal — two secret flavourings.

Way it works is, you light your Premier and inhale — just the way you would a non-multi-million-dollar ciggie. This draws hot air past the aluminum capsule, which vaporizes the glycerin and nicotine in the dried tobacco beads. It also activates those two aforementioned secret flavourings. The whole miasmic mess then passes through two, count 'em, two, filters and into the smoker's mouth and lungs.

Quite revolutionary, really. Premier produces almost no tar, which means it's less likely to cause lung cancer. It gives off almost no external smoke, which means it's less likely to cause black eyes and broken noses from outraged non-smokers around you.

There's just the one tiny problem with the new, healthier, $325 million Premier cigarette. It tastes bad. Awful, in fact. In test marketings, buyers would buy a pack, smoke one, give away the rest and never buy them again.

Sounds to me like my first cigarette. It tasted awful, too. And well it might. It was made of pine needles wrapped in toilet paper. But unlike Premiers, it didn't cost $325 million. Take out inflation and it sounds to me like the smoking business has just come full circle.

Or is that a smoke ring?

The Rolls-Royce of Pocket Knives

IN THAT CLASSIC movie *The Third Man*, there's a scene where Orson Welles delivers the ultimate free enterprise speech. It goes: "In Italy, for thirty years under the Borgias, they had warfare, terror, murder and bloodshed, but they produced Michelangelo, Leonardo da Vinci and the Renaissance. In Switzerland, they had brotherly love, they had 500 years of democracy and peace — and what did they produce? The cuckoo clock."

Poor old Switzerland. Take away the picture postcard mountains and what have you got? Toronto. The Swiss have long been perceived as bland, boring and monotonous — and unfairly so, I think.

After all, was it not the Swiss who gave us that magic talisman lusted after by every North American male from sprout-size cub scout to aging yuppie?

I refer, of course, to the Swiss Army knife. A utensil that stands out among common pocket knives as a Rolls-Royce Silver Ghost would stand out in a fleet of Checker cabs.

The Swiss Army knife is the red one with the white cross emblazoned on its flank. But that's just the outside of the knife — it's the innards that separate the Swiss Army from all the other buck, barlow, pen, jack and clasp knives.

Packing a Swiss Army knife is like carrying a toolbox in your hip pocket. Even the simplest model gives you a nail file, tweezers, scissors and a toothpick along with the knife blade. But if you really want to get into it, you can order the SwissChamp — which has twenty-nine "blades" — or, for terminal gadget freaks, the SOS model which boasts forty fold-out features, including a ball-point pen, a fish scaler, a wood saw and a magnifying glass.

Apparently a lot of North Americans do want to get into it. Last year we bought more than $25 million worth of the little red gizmos.

The Swiss have been making the knives for nearly a hundred years, but the first time they showed up in North America was in the kitbags of Canadian and American soldiers returning from Europe after World War II. Hungry for European souvenirs, our guys had bought or swapped for them with Swiss soldiers. Since everybody in the Swiss Army seemed to carry one, our soldiers dubbed them "Swiss Army knives." The name stuck.

The North American love affair with the Swiss import shows no signs of abating. Victorinox Cutlery of Switzerland now pumps out sixty different models of the Swiss Army knife and the U.S. market alone sucks up 35 per cent of them.

The question is why? Why are all we soft-palmed, pudgy-bellied, by-and-large urban guys buying a tool that theoretically only Robinson Crusoe could need?

Be honest — when's the last time you grabbed your pocket knife to scale a lake trout, strip an electrical wire or to read the fine print in your mortgage?

Have you ever actually tried to *use* the wood-saw blade in a Swiss Army knife? I have. Yesterday, as an experiment, I decided to "fell" a poplar about five inches in diameter out behind my place, using only my knife.

I did it, but it took a long time and left me with two blisters on my palm. I think I could've managed it a little faster if I'd just used my teeth.

So why do we keep buying them? Because we're romantics. There is a segment of the Canadian male populace, the members of which are Truly Handy. They can set the timing on their lawnmowers, find studs in the wall, mix cement, put up wallpaper and barbecue a steak to perfection. There are precisely thirty-seven such Canadian males and they wouldn't think of buying a Swiss Army knife.

The rest of us are technological nerds. Woody Allen is our patron saint. We can barely change a lightbulb or remember which key goes in the ignition. We buy the Swiss Army knives because we think they give us an edge.

They don't, of course. What they give is a huge belly laugh to those thirty-seven Truly Handy guys. They also provide a tidy income to the Swiss gnomes who keep selling them to us.

Ah, the Swiss: they may be bland and monotonous — but they ain't stupid.

Running Shoe
Run-around

IT'S INTERESTING HOW tiny, trivial things can sometimes thread themselves through the whole tapestry of your life. Take running shoes. Running shoes are responsible for my first sense of being a Canadian. Must have been thirty-five years ago on a dock in Muskoka. I remember this loud blond brush-cut teenager with an accent that sounded like a speech impediment wearing a shiny new pair of strange-looking running shoes with little rubber discs on the ankles. He was bragging about his brand-new "sneakahs."

"Sneakers?" I thought, what is this guy — a cat burglar?

Naw. He was just an American. Americans called them sneakers; we called them running shoes. I kinda preferred the name sneakers, but I stubbornly continued to call them running shoes. Patriotism sometimes roots in pretty sandy soil.

Mind you, none of us had much running-shoe imagination back then. Not like today.

We just had the standard-issue, rubber-bottom, canvas-top $6.98 shoes that laced up to the ankle and lasted from first mud till the snow flew again. Today? Phew. I spent part of yesterday afternoon window-shopping in a downtown shoe store. An *athletic* . . . shoe store. They've got court shoes, tennis shoes, jogging shoes and sprinting shoes. They've got aerobics shoes and warm-up shoes, track shoes and cycling shoes. They've even got an entire line of walking shoes — which you would think would have to represent full circle for the athletic shoe business, but I doubt it. Don't sell these merchandising guys short. I expect any day to walk by that store window and see the all new Napping Shoe —

revolutionary footwear that fights fallen arches and corrects pigeon toes while you doze in front of the TV.

Mind you, it's not all advertising hype. Modern running shoes are a far technological cry from my old $6.98 blacktops.

The old gum rubber soles are gone, replaced by an amalgam of carbon and rubber in tread patterns more elaborate than Maori tattoos. The old floppy canvas tops are a thing of the past, too. Modern "uppers" use suede, plastic foam and nylon mesh to create a shoe that's much stronger and yet lighter than the smelly old blacktops at the back of my memory closet. And that's not all. The new running shoes feature special reinforced heels, patented mid-sole shock absorbers and all manner of gizmos to make runners run faster and more comfortably. Tiger Brand shoes feature a gel insert to absorb the thump of feet hitting the ground. I've got a pair of shoes here that have air capsules under the heel to do the same thing. All this is not, of course, included in the old $6.98 price. Actually, you can get a pretty brisk cardiovascular workout just reading the price tags on these new running shoes.

Know what the irony is? Know what all these flotation devices and miracle fibres and kinetic wedges are trying to recreate? Something that world-famous runners like Kipoge Keno, Zola Budd and gold-medal marathon runner Abede Bikila discovered a long time ago. That when it comes to running, nothing beats the efficiency of . . . bare feet. Those runners all run in their bare feet.

Which of course come a lot cheaper. Cheaper even than $6.98.

Jeff Craig,
Call Home!

THIS ESSAY CAN BE considered to be an All-Points Bulletin. Its message is simple. Boiled down to five essential words it would read:

Jeff Craig, come home immediately.

Back when life was simple, Jeff lived just down the street from me. He's a cheerful, good-looking young guy in his mid-twenties going through the Gypsy stage of his journalism career, flitting from newspaper to newspaper — writing a column here, covering city hall there, taking over the duties of editor somewhere else, then packing up his notepads and his *Roget's Thesaurus* and moving on to some other more attractive newspaper just over the ink-smudged rainbow. Last I heard he was deep in the wilds of northeastern Ontario, churning out copy for the *Temiskaming Tribune* or the *Cobalt Chronicle-Journal* or maybe it was the *Porcupine Times Picayune.*

Doesn't matter. I tell you all that by way of background, in case you spot the guy on the street. The reason Jeff Craig must be apprehended and returned to my neighbourhood immediately is because Jeff Craig is one other thing.

A computer genius.

More to the point, he's the computer genius who convinced me that my life would be transformed and my writing revivified if only I bought a Tandy 1000 EX Floppy Disc 640 Megabyte PC with Accessory Hard Disc Drive and RGB Color Monitor CM-5.

Looking back now, I realize I didn't truly need the aforementioned. I was reasonably happy punching out my column on the old dented Olympia portable typewriter I'd been hunched over for years. True, the space bar seemed to be suffering from a touch of bursitis, and I couldn't write any sentences that called for a capital *Q*, but we were like an old married couple, my Olympia and me — well past the ecstasies of the honeymoon, but comfortable with each other.

Comfortable until Jeff Craig came along, anyway.

Jeff is an exceedingly polite chap, but I'm certain I saw the flicker of a smirk cross his face when he discovered I still worked on a typewriter. He said nothing — merely showed me his state-of-the-art personal computer. It was like handing the ignition keys of a Lamborghini to a guy who'd been driving a ten-year-old Volkswagen Bug. I was hooked. Within hours I was negotiating a second mortgage on the house and selling my firstborn into slavery in order to arrange financing on my very own personal computer.

Jeff Craig supervised the buying of the grey plastic modules that were my keyboard, my monitor, my disc drive and my printer. Jeff Craig came home with me, hooked up all the wires and thinggummees to the proper doohickeys and whatchamacallits. Jeff Craig taught me important PC words like "format," "cursor" and "MS-DOS."

Then Jeff Craig moved away.

To be honest, I was having such fun with my new toy that I scarcely noticed he was gone for the first few days.

Then my computer turned on me.

It was subtle at first. Curt little messages like NOT A VALID FILE crept onto my screen. Soon it was issuing orders in gibberish like ENTER Y TO DOWNLOAD FONTS, N TO SKIP, ESC TO CANCEL and delivering doom-laden ultimatums like CANNOT SAVE FILE or LIST IS EMPTY.

My local computer store was no help. They speak only Egyptian there. "Why didn't you punch in the A>copyA:***/B command?" they ask me disgustedly.

My computer is in full mutiny now. It lets me type out anything I want on the screen, then eats it right before my eyes. Does anybody else have a computer that snickers? Mine does. Come home, Jeff Craig, and make it behave again.

I had to use my backup system to get this essay out. It's a cordless, laptop manual word processor with infinite megabyte capacity that comes with its own data obliterator on the opposite end of the unit.

I think we used to call them pencils.

Don't Call Me;
I Won't Call You

HERE'S A NEWS STORY I wouldn't have minded living without: Canadian scientists have come up with the technology to allow airplane passengers to dial directly to virtually any telephone on earth. That's right — it is now possible for you, peering queasily 36,000 feet down from window seat 12A, to eavesdrop as your portly fellow passenger in 12B jaws intimately with his wife, his kids, his partner, his creditors and/or his mother-in-law.

Great. The Muzak, the Pygmy seat, the treacherous hair-trigger chairback tray, the flash-burned feather or leather dinner, the sheer incongruity of being there in an outsized aluminum cigar tube six miles over Sault Ste. Marie with a *Report on Business* on your lap — that's not enough. Now we have to have inflight telephone calls.

Frankly, I find it depressing. Airplanes were one of my last refuges from Ma Bell. Used to be able to hide in my car, too, but they took that away a couple of years back when they perfected the cellular phone.

Perfected? Did I say perfected? I consider the cellular phone to be sheer demon spawn — the most diabolical innovation since the creation of the back-hooked bra. Cellular car phones have immeasurably increased the chances that the last thing you and I will ever see on this earth is the grille of an errant oncoming automobile, and behind that a driver with one hand on the wheel, the other hand dialling.

Call me selfish, but I don't want to go out in a head-on with some yuppie squawking "Sell!" to his broker.

Last time the *Guinness Book of Records* did a count, there were

285,723,398 telephones in the world. Nearly 286 million! That's better than ten phones for every Canadian man, woman and child! And soon, thanks to Canadian technology, there will be even more of them. The new ones will hover overhead like electronic gyr falcons waiting to pounce on some fat ptarmigan of a non-ringing telephone like mine. Or yours.

Now that the Wichita Lineman is wiring up the heavens, are there any places left to hide? Not many. I suppose the summit of K2 and the storm-tossed waters off Cape Horn are still one-ringy-dingy-two-ringy-dingy free . . . but that's a long way to go for a little peace and quiet. We could always pull an undergraduate Dustin Hoffman, strap on some scuba tanks and settle at the deep end of the pool, but what's that good for . . . a couple of hours, tops? Plus, you come out looking like a bleached prune.

Nope, I think the only possible solution to creeping telephon-ism is massive passive resistance. And I think it makes sense to start with the newest telephone offensive (and I mean offen-sive) — this phone-in-the-sky thing.

Let's you and me cut a deal: I promise not to phone you from Air Canada Flight 349 . . . if you promise to return the favour. Agreed? Swell.

And remember our slogan — stolen from a song title by Jimmy Buffet: "If your phone doesn't ring, it's me."

Rust in Pieces

D UNNO HOW IT IS in your life, but cocaine is not the main addictive chemical in mine. Neither is marijuana or hashish, . . . angel dust or ecstasy. I go whole weeks without a passing thought to heroin or opium, LSD or TCP, bennies, reds, uppers, downers . . . as for Qualuudes, I'm not even sure if I'm spelling it correctly.

No, the chemical that's got me hooked right now is something I can pick up right off the street every day. Matter of fact, that's the very best way to get it — right off the street. It's sodium chloride. Or, as it's known to denizens of the motoring underworld . . . road salt.

It's a lot cheaper to buy than crack or smack. My local roads department gives the stuff away. It's out there just lying on the pavement, and you don't even have to pick it up. Just drive your car down the street after a couple of inches of snow falls. Road salt will come to *you.*

To your car, anyway. Actually, I lied when I said that I'm addicted to road salt. I'm not — and neither is my car. But somebody up there is. My car pays the physical price. I pick up the financial tab.

As do you — even if you don't own a car. Road salt doesn't just turn my buggy into the automotive equivalent of a terminal opium junkie. It also attacks road surfaces and roadside trees, farm crops, overpasses, underpasses and of course every other car, truck, bus and moped that dips a wheel in it.

The folks who put the salt on our roads argue that a little bit of rust is a lot cheaper than 10,000 fender-benders and bumperthumpers every time the heavens dust us with a couple of centimetres of white stuff. And they have a point. In that great swatch of Canada that gets a lot of freeze-thaw, freeze-thaw flip-flops over the winter months, salt gets rid of dangerous ice and snow on the roads quite quickly. Sand or gravel won't do the trick, and with the demise of wood and coal stoves there just aren't enough ashes and cinders to go around anymore.

Oh, science *has* come up with a chemical compound that will melt ice effectively without leaving our vehicles looking as if they'd been machine-gunned by an Al Fatah death squad, then dipped in a vat of muriatic acid. Only one small problem with the miracle chemical compound. It costs $1,000 a ton. Rock salt costs forty.

So is that it? Do we Canucks just have to resign ourselves to an eternity of winters watching our cars decompose in our driveways?

Maybe not. A Toronto company by the name of Canadian Protective Products Incorporated has come up with a product called Freezguard + PCI — it's a salt combined with a rust inhibitor that is 80 per cent less corrosive than the rock salt we use now. Mind you, it costs $100 a ton, more than twice as much as rock salt. But that's cheap when you consider the hundreds of millions of dollars in damage road salt does every year.

So, good news for Canadian motorists down the road . . . but not this year. For this winter it's more of the same: road salt. And one more reason to yearn for spring, when the geese fly overhead, the robins come home to nest, the goldfinches shed their winter plumage, and our cars get the chance to go cold turkey.

Deadly Toys for Big Boys

Cars are built for speed, and highways are built for speed. What is not built for speed is the human body.

U.S. TRANSPORTATION DEPARTMENT OFFICIAL

I told my people that when I stepped down on the throttle, I want to be scared.

FRED SCHAAFSMA, ENGINEER

A S CHIEF ENGINEER of the Corvette division of General Motors, Fred Schaafsma is in a position to get pretty much what he wants, automobile-wise. You can get it, too — the Corvette ZR-1. Three hundred and seventy-five horsepower under the hood. Capable of going from zero to sixty miles an hour in four seconds.

To be fair to the folks at Chevrolet, the new Corvette isn't the only absurdly overpowered buggy you'll be dodging when the snow melts. A magazine ad for Honda's Acura Legend Coupe boasts "Even the interior was designed at 125 miles per hour." A television commercial for BMW's M6 sedan calls it "a most elegant argument for tripling the national speed limit."

And you've probably seen the TV promo for Porsche that purrs, "For lunch it prefers Ferraris, although it has been known to snack on Corvettes."

There's just one small problem with all these wheeled rockets the car makers are pumping out — nobody this side of the Mosport racetrack needs them. There is not a public road on this continent on which you can legally drive at 125 miles an hour — and how often do you need to get from a dead stop to a mile a minute in four seconds? I don't know about you, but I'm just three points away from a polite *tête-à-tête* with the local gendarmerie regarding my propensity for showing up on their radar guns — and my car couldn't get from zero to sixty over a long weekend.

But whether we need 'em or not, the new supercharged cars are here. Our highways can't handle them, and neither, five'll get you ten, can the amateurs who'll be buying them. But they're here: big shiny toys for man-children who believe a certain combination of chrome, rubber, steel, fiberglass and an internal combustion engine will transform them into Lawrences of Arabia.

We've been down this highway before. Back in the sixties when much of the citizenry was into headbands and flower power, the knuckle-dragging segment was buying GTOs and Shelby Mustangs. Muscle cars. Bulging behemoths that looked like ordinary cars pumped up on steroids. They guzzled gas like 747s, but they were undeniably powerful.

And popular — at least among those members of the populace who breathe through their mouths, lean to a diet of beer and pizza and have LOVE and HATE tattooed on their knuckles.

Those muscle cars went fast, all right. A lot of them stopped even faster — fast enough to send their occupants through the windshield and the insurance rates for muscle cars right through the roof. That, as well as the Great Gas Scare, drove the muscle cars to the brink of extinction.

But not over, alas. They're back. Oh, they're not calling them muscle cars this time around. The image-makers are going for sleek and elegant instead of bulgy and menacing — Wayne Gretzky over Mike Tyson, if you will. But they are muscle cars by any other name. Cars that, as an old sea captain would put it, carry way too much sail for the size of the craft.

As muscle cars, they will inevitably do what they were designed to do. They will go too fast and some of them will go out of control and crash, killing and maiming a whole lot of people who perhaps right this moment are falling under the spell of those slick, beguiling television commercials.

But you don't have to own a muscle car to get hit by one. A lot of us will have a rendezvous with those cars that we wouldn't wish on our worst enemy.

Maybe you. Maybe me.

Maybe Fred Schaafsma.

I don't know if Fred's scared, but I am.

Do Not Go Unpickled into That Good Night

L ET'S BE MORBID for a moment — what's your favourite death
scene?

Wolfe and Montcalm?

Romeo and Juliet?

Jimmy Cagney on the water tower?

Well, I hate to be flip, but I think my all-time favourite death
scene is the one in the pet shop where Monty Pythoner John
Cleese tries to get his money back for a Norwegian Blue lying
talons-up on the counter. The I-want-my-money-back eulogy
goes, you may remember, like this:

"It's passed on. This parrot is no more. It has ceased to be. It's
expired and gone to see its maker. This is a late parrot. It's a stiff.
Bereft of life. It rests in peace. If you hadn't nailed it to the perch
it would be pushing up the daisies. It's rung down the curtain and
joined the choir invisible. *This* is an ex-parrot."

Death scenes don't come much more final than that.

But that's the problem with death. It isn't really final. A person
or a parrot may kick off, but the business of death goes on.
Disposal of the body, for instance. There are choices to be made.
Cremation? Burial at sea? Simple interment on a grassy knoll
overlooking a Norwegian fiord? Decisions, decisions.

And it's getting more complex, this business of afterlife parking.
There's a company in California that offers to freeze your body
indefinitely . . . in the hope that someday science will be clever
enough to thaw you out and put you on the road again. There's a
fellow in Florida who's trying to sign up folks who would like to

have their earthly remains sealed in a space capsule and shot into orbit. Chilling prospect: the possibility of going out in the evening to watch the sunset and Uncle Alfred go by.

Last week a brand-new post-mortem option unveiled itself. For $8,000, a Salt Lake City company will . . . take my body, soak it in solution of phenol and formaldehyde for a few days and . . . well, remember those frogs you got to work on in Grade 10 Biology? Yeah.

Eight thousand bucks to get pickled in Salt Lake City.

You have to wonder why anybody would do it. Formaldehyde doesn't do a thing for your complexion. Those frogs didn't look good, floating around in those bottles.

And it's not even new, as thrills go. It's just a chemical variation on the indignities offered to the body of King Tutankhamen 3,500 years ago.

I don't know about you, but I wouldn't relish the prospect of spending eternity in a mason jar — or as headliner at the Royal Ontario Museum. I think I'll take a pass on this opportunity of a deathtime.

Not that any of us can expect to escape the rigors of life entirely. It goes on. As Johnny Carson points out, "For three days after death, hair and fingernails continue to grow. But phone calls taper off."

Big Brother Is Reading Your Wrist

B ACK IN THE NINETEENTH CENTURY, North American Indians were introduced to the science of photography.

It was a marriage that almost didn't take.

Photographers were surprised to learn that when they pointed their cameras at Sioux braves or Apache chiefs, the subjects responded by pointing arrows, spears and the odd Winchester 30-30 right back at the photographer.

The Indians weren't striking dramatic poses. They regarded cameras with about the same affection the Ayatollah would have for an autographed copy of *The Satanic Verses*, which is to say they loathed the things. They believed that the camera could steal their spirits.

We've come a long way, Kemosabe.

Nowadays we don't much worry about the threat of cameras stealing our souls. We line up for the privilege of having our photos affixed to drivers' licences and company ID cards. Dentists and doctors regularly shoot X-ray photos of impacted molars and twisted ankles. Automatic TV cameras routinely pan across whole shuffling hordes of us in banks, public washrooms and shopping malls. Even the corner store has a Big Brother eyeball mounted up in the ceiling. I'm on TV every time I drop in to buy a bag of two per cent.

And there's more to come. If you find it offensive having a Rent-a-Cop run a metal wand under your armpits and over your privates every time you try to board a plane, chances are you're

176

really going to have trouble with the newest wrinkle in the security game — an innovation called Veincheck.

Veincheck is a brand-new security system for credit cards. The people in charge have decided that signatures are too easy to forge and fingerprints are too easy to steal. Accordingly, someday soon when you get to the checkout counter with your goodies and throw down your charge card, you may be asked to hold out your wrist.

The checkout person will then take a picture of the back of your hand.

Kinky? Nope. The camera is scanning the subcutaneous veins in your hand and translating that pattern into digital information that is stored on the back of your charge card.

If what the camera sees doesn't match with what's imprinted on your card, it means you're using that charge card illegally.

Chances are at this point they'll ask you to hold out your other wrist as well.

To facilitate the fitting of handcuffs.

Veincheck fits right in with another hi-tech security system that's already being used in some exclusive circles where controlled access is crucial. It's called Eyedentification. With this one, a low-intensity scanner looks right into your eyeballs and reads the pattern of blood vessels on your retina. Such patterns are, the experts say, like snowflakes — no two alike. Therefore, if your retinal blood vessels don't check out, you don't get past security.

Veincheck is still in the experimental stage, and Eyedentification is used primarily to control access to high-security establishments and to keep track of prison inmates. But there's no reason to suppose that such systems couldn't proliferate and find their way into just about every corner of your life. Indeed, Joe Rice, the man who invented Veincheck, says he can see the day coming when you and I could program virtually everything we own — car, front door, television, VCR, checking account, motorboat at the cottage — to operate only when activated by a card that recognizes the vein patterns on the back of the owner's hand.

Revolutionary? Well, I suppose. But I keep thinking of that old Charlton Heston sci-fi movie — the one about some Futureworld where every citizen has a silicon "information" chip implanted in his wrist at birth.

And I keep remembering those Indians and their aversion to having their pictures taken.

I suspect those "underdeveloped aboriginals" sensed something we're much too sophisticated to understand.

Gun One

With all the violence and murder and killings we've
had in the United States, I think you will agree that
we must keep firearms from people who have no
business with them.

AH, YES. WAS THERE ever a phenomenon quite as bizarre as
America's ongoing love affair with personal firearms? Year
in, year out, hundreds of thousands of Americans find themselves
staring at the business end of a handgun. Twenty-two thousand
die from the encounter annually. A huge percentage of the remain-
der are crippled and scarred for life. Doctors, nurses, even law-
enforcement officers look at the daily carnage and shake their
heads in disbelief. Occasionally, some braver-than-average American like the one quoted above will clear his throat and ask if it
isn't about time the U.S. joined the rest of the civilized world in
restricting access to firearms. Whereupon America, like some
punch-drunk barroom brawler, shakes its head, lifts its face out of
the sawdust and growls, "Whut? Take away our constitooshunul
right tuh bear arms? No way, Hoss!"

And that's it! No more discussion. Nobody wants to hear how
there are more gun homicides in the city of Washington in one
month than there are in Great Britain in one year. Don't try to tell
Yankees that more of their countrymen have been shot by each
other than were gunned down by all the German, North Korean
and Viet Cong soldiers put together. Americans just flat-out love
their shootin' irons.

It's a love that gets expressed in odd ways. Designer handguns
for the little lady, for instance. Smith & Wesson has just launched
a petite pistol called "The Ladysmith." It comes in tasteful frosted-
blue steel with its own colour-coordinated clutch-bag carrying

case. Last spring, Miami hosted the Bing Bang Boom gun show —
a fashion show on how to wear concealed weapons. "We're trying
to show the contemporary woman that she can carry a concealed
weapon and still look good," said a spokesman.

Of course, it doesn't really matter how you look if you happen
to be strolling by Lindbergh Junior High School in Long Beach,
California — the kids inside won't be able to see you, anyway.
That's because of the new, nine-foot-high concrete wall that runs
between the school and a nearby housing project. Purpose of the
wall: to stop bullets. Gunfire from drug dealers and other assorted
street scum in the nearby project has threatened the lives of kids
and teachers at the school. Not long ago a student playing basket-
ball in the schoolyard was shot in the chest and nearly died. That's
when they decided to turn Lindbergh Junior High into a fort.

"It's really sad that something like this has to be done," says
principal Max Faley, "but it's needed in today's society."

Maybe in your society, Max, but not in mine.

Americans who try to change their insane gun-control laws find
themselves staring down the well-oiled muzzle of the National
Rifle Association. The NRA cranks out a steady stream of advertisements that play up every American's "patriotic right" to own a
lethal weapon. The association also lavishes megabucks on key
Washington lobbyists to snarl and suffocate any impending gun-
control legislation.

America's gun-happiness doesn't have much to do with logic.
Recent history has seen the near-shooting of president Ford, the
wounding of president Reagan and the murder of president Kennedy. You'd think that kind of bloodstained legacy would make
the presidency very keen on gun control, right? Not on your
snub-nose. President Bush (a card-carrying member of the NRA
himself) recently refused to ban the sale of semi-automatic weapons.

Mind you, the U.S. did come down hard on lawn darts. Over
the past ten years, three people have been killed by errant lawn
darts. In the same decade nearly a quarter of a million Americans
have been killed by guns. Lawn darts are banned; semi-automatic
weapons are swell.

Make any sense to you?

Oh, that fellow I quoted at the beginning of this column? He made that speech just five days before his rendezvous with a scruffy drifter in a Los Angeles hotel kitchen. The drifter was carrying an 8-shot, .22 caliber Iver Johnson in a brown paper lunch bag.

The other guy's name was Bobby Kennedy.

Something to Chew On

ANYBODY OUT THERE remember Lonny Donegan? He was a Cockney singer back in the sixties who had a string — make that a thread — of novelty hit tunes on the pop charts. "My Old Man's a Dustman" — that was one. Then there was the Lonny Donegan tune that featured perhaps the longest title in the history of pop music — a title that was also the first line of the song. It went "Does yourrrrrrrr chewing gum lose its flavour on the bedpost overnight?"

Got to thinking about Lonny Donegan's jaw-wrenching tribute to chewing gum when I read in the paper last week that scientists in Chicago are in fact hunched over their lab tables and toiling away on that very question — why does chewing gum lose its flavour, and what can be done about it? They hope to at least double the length of time that elapses between that first fragrant chomp and the point at which your gum begins to taste like extract of inner tube.

Well, I say good luck to them. Chewing gum's occupied far too important a cranny in my life — and I daresay in yours — to be wadded up and flung into the wastebasket of history. Think of the taste memories alone. Fleers Double Bubble. Black Jack. Thrills. Remember Thrills? Twelve purple pellets in a yellow-and-white package? Tasted like soap, and turned your tongue the colour of a Concord grape, but I couldn't resist them.

Ah, yes, and Beeman's Beechnut gum . . . and of course Clorets. Clorets was what happened when gum turned serious. It cost more than ordinary gum, but then it did so much more. In my time no savvy teenager would think of going on a first date without investing in a package of Clorets. And the toughs who loitered around the school parking lot during lunch hour chewed Clorets by the carload because it masked the smell of tobacco on their breath.

Truth is, Clorets masked the smell of just about everything — masked it with the overpowering smell of Clorets. Which meant that anyone who chewed Clorets was automatically assumed to be just returning from a smoke break. Or a heavy date.

Ah, but chewing gum goes way back beyond even my high school days. When Europeans first stumbled ashore in North America, they found natives chewing on spruce gum. I've tried it. It will never replace Trident. In 1870, a Staten Island photographer and part-time inventor by the name of Thomas Adams finally gave up trying to come up with a rubber substitute. He was using sap from a Mexican tree called the zapodilla. Nothing worked. That's it, he thought. Forget it. I quit. Idly, he popped a chunk of the goo in his mouth and started to chew.

And bellowed, "*Yom yoom yumph!*" Which is what "Eureka!" sounds like when you say it with a mouth full of zapodilla sap.

Thomas Adams had just created the chewing-gum business. If he'd spoken better Spanish he might have done it a whole lot sooner. Mexicans had been chewing that stuff free for centuries. They called it "chicle." Thomas Adams made it commercial and that's how the world got chewing gum. Beginning with . . . Adam's Chiclets.

Outwitting the Smart House

A S A NEW HOMEOWNER, I sensed I was over my head when the guy from Waterfun World asked, "So, how's your solar system?"

I realized what he was talking about — that Rube Goldbergian goiter of pipes and plastic panels encrusted on the roof of the pool cabana like some strange creeping infestation. He meant, "How's your solar-heating system working?" I knew that. Part of me did, anyway. But the other, overwrought and highly paranoid portion of my mind seized on his actual words and Ping-Ponged them back and forth across my brain pan.

How's my solar system? *How's my solar system?* Isn't that a question that can properly be addressed only to God?

There you have my dilemma in a nutshell. Some guy tries to pass the time of day with a little nuts-and-bolts gossip, and I panic and turn it into some kind of cosmic query.

My problem is I can't *do* nuts and bolts — or bits and bytes. I'm a caveman. Well, that's a tad harsh — a log-cabin man, say, adrift in a neverending suburb of sidesplits and duplexes, town houses and ranch styles, condos and A-frames. I live in a world full of magical domiciles that are in turn crammed with voodooistic totems — microwaves and VCRs, electric-eye garage doors and refrigerators that talk back to me — and I understand none of it.

Actually, there are quite a few of us around. We bite a lot of nails, watch a lot of Woody Allen movies and try to land jobs where we can earn enough money to pay handy people to do our dirty work.

By and large, we mind our own business and try to stay out of the path of the rolling technological juggernaut, but every once in a while we get the grandiose notion that we can cope. Then we do foolish things like buying a Black and Decker WorkMate or investing in a wine-making kit.

Or buying a house that's too smart for us.

"You're going to love this place," purred the real estate agent. "It's got an electronic security system, a soft-water system — why, the pool's even got its own solar system."

Solar system? Isn't that . . .

I should have run back to my downtown, fourteenth-floor, all-utilities-included apartment, but I didn't. In the grip of my own grandiose notion, I bought the place. But only after I insisted that the former owner take me and my trusty tape recorder on a walking, talking tour of every joist and stud in the place. He did, and I taped every word. Just in time, too, because the ex-owner left on a world cruise the next week. I figure his ship was off the Azores about the time I discovered the tapes we'd made were blank.

Play *and* Record. When am I going to learn that you have to press Play *and* Record?

Since I'm trying to give up whining, I won't regale you with details of how the electric eye went quite literally on the blink and locked me in the garage for two hours. I won't go on about the day I found myself up to my armpits in foam down in the basement, thanks to a malfunctioning soft-water system. I won't bore you with my explanation (which the cops found so hilarious) about how (once again) my dog's wagging tail had set off the Armageddon siren wail of the security system. A system that while it is shredding the tympanic membranes of household residents, simultaneously (and irrevocably) alerts the police station, the fire department and three neighbours, none of whom even nod at me anymore.

The point is, there comes a time when even wimps must strike back. I may not know how to connect with the modern world, but by cracky, I still know how to disconnect. Off switches are Off switches and wall plugs are wall plugs.

Today my garage door opens and closes with a hefty manual tug, the way garage doors are supposed to open and close. My security system is the aforementioned tail-wagger that barks infrequently, but not loud enough to summon the law or bother the neighbours. I drink my water hard, and if that coats the pipes, domestic and internal, so be it.

And my solar system? I shut it off, too. Nowadays my swimming pool just lies there *au naturel*, sucking up whatever sunshine there is — sort of like Grenadier Pond, Lake Ontario and the Atlantic.

I figure if it's good enough for The Big Guy, it's good enough for me.

E-fish-iency
Experts

*The gods do not deduct from man's allotted span
the hours spent in fishing.*

ANCIENT BABYLONIAN PROVERB

A H, YES, THE NOBLE ART of angling. Just a fisherman, his gear and a wily trout lurking in a shaded pool around the next river bend. I've always been half in love with the idea of fishing, though I've never been much good at it. The trout was always a little too wily for me. So, come to that, were the pickerel, pike, perch and bass — be they largemouth, smallmouth, silver or rock. I may be a fishing failure, but I love the peacefulness of the sport. And the mystery of it. Every couple of years I dust off my old tackle box, dab a little Three-In-One on my spincasting reel and try my luck again.

But after what I saw at an outdoor show last week, something tells me I may have drowned my last worm. It was one of those What's-New-on-the-Water exhibitions — everything from bus-length motor launches to thumbnail-size fishing lures. Normally I would enjoy a show like that, but this one bummed me out. I came out of it thinking that if I was a fish I would turn in my fins right now. The age-old contest between angler and anglee has been tilted on its head. Thanks to modern technology, the fish hasn't got a prayer.

Remember when fishing was a barefoot kid with a bamboo pole and a tin can full of worms? Let me introduce you to the Ryobi America Baitcaster. If you've got $125 you can strap this reel onto your fishing rod and check the *digital readouts* every time you make a cast. The Ryobi America Baitcaster is computerized to keep track of the line going out and makes adjustments to make sure you don't get backlashes and snarls. For a few more bucks

187

you can pick up a Daiwa spinning reel that'll print out your foot-per-second rate of casting and reeling in. But heck, why not shoot the works and buy yourself a Cannon Digi-Troll? It's only $695 U.S., and when you slap this baby on your rod it'll automatically drop your trolling lure to any pre-set depth. Not only that — it'll raise or lower the lure automatically until it finds fish.

Speaking of finding fish . . . .

I hate to be tiresomely romantic, but fishing to me is two people casting off opposite sides of a rowboat in the pre-dawn mist of a northern lake with only the plop of the lures and perhaps the eerie ululations of a loon by way of noise. What fishing is *not* is a thirty-foot, hundred-plus horsepowered, fibreglass-hulled floating battle station that approaches fishing as a search-and-destroy mission.

The new fishing boats have to be seen to be believed. They come with depth finders to locate and pinpoint those lake or river-bottom holes that fish might be hiding in. They carry temperature gauges that can track down underground springs where fish might gather on a muggy afternoon. They boast pH meters that a fisherman can drop over the side to measure the water acidity at various depths. (Fish like to feed in certain concentrations of acidity, you see.)

Then, of course, there's the *pièce de resistance*, angling technologywise — the fish finder itself. It's about the size of a tackle box and it works just like submarine sonar. It sends sound waves down into the water. When they hit something solid — like, say, a school of trophy-size lake trout — the waves bounce back to the boat, are recorded and printed out on a graph. Hey, presto, Joe Angler knows exactly where to put his baited hook.

The new gear takes the guesswork out of fishing, but it creates one tiny problem.

We're running out of fish. We've loaded the odds in favour of the angler so much that it's now possible to fish out a river or a small lake in a single season. Says one avid angler, "In three or four years, there may be no fish."

No problem for the modern-day, hi-tech "sports" fishermen, though — they'll just switch to another sport.

Like, maybe, shooting ducks in a barrel.

PART 6
The Things That Get Us

Code id da Nodes

WANNA HEAR ONE of the all-time stupidest phrases in the entire English language?

"I caught a cold."

I *have* a cold. I did not "catch" it. I may have tripped over it on a bus, picked it up from some disreputable Bell telephone mouthpiece or been bushwacked by it near the punch bowl at the New Year's party . . . but I did not "catch" it. If anything, it caught me.

What's more, there's nothing cold about my cold. Getting a cold has nothing to do with getting cold. Check it out. Shuck off all your clothes, throw open the front door, go out on the front lawn and wallow in a snowbank for twenty minutes. You may get pneumonia, chillblains, frostbite, bronchitis, sinusitis and a lifetime membership in the Polar Bear Club, but you will not get the common cold. For that you have to run afoul of a miserable little critter called coryza.

Coryza is a virus, and all you need to know about him is that he's small, he's tough . . . and he loves you. Coryza's idea of the ultimate swell time is to bivouac in the back of your throat and go mano-a-mano with your white corpuscles until you run out of Kleenex or he's forced to say uncle to antihistamines.

And don't hold your rasping breath for that to happen. The only commodity that exceeds the array of disgusting cold symptoms is the array of pathetic and ineffectual cold remedies. "Eat lots of onions," my mother said. Well, that cuts down the frequency of transmission, what with the rest of the human race reeling back from the odiferous force field you've created. But onions do not prevent or kill a cold.

190

And neither do megadoses of vitamin C, and I don't care if Linus Pauling did win the Nobel Prize. Listen: I dropped so many tabs of C this winter that I've got a rash under my navel that spells out Sunkist.

I also still have my cold.

Neighbour suggests sitting in a cold bath — cleverly hitting on the one thing that I think would be worse than having a cold.

"I gargle with whiskey several times a day," said W. C. Fields, "and I haven't had a cold in years."

True, but he did have a dessicated liver, blackouts, DTs and a schnoz that looked like a pomegranate strung with Christmas lights.

The sad fact is, there is no cure for the common cold. We know how to swap hearts and lungs, we routinely lob live humans into space and reel them back. We easily design vest-pocket micro-computers and continent-wide water diversions . . . but we do it with dripping noses and rheumy eyes and scratchy gullets. Stop a forest fire? Right away. Wipe out polio and yellow fever? Before lunch. Cure the common cold? Gee, sorry. Pull up the covers, drink plenty of liquids and keep your trigger finger on the Kleenex box.

Doctors are a big help. Mine told me that if I placed myself in his care, he should be able to clear my cold up within a week . . . whereas without his help it might hold on for as long as seven days.

I sneezed on him.

Laugh? I Thought I'd Diet

M Y WAR AGAINST fat began one day in a radio studio high above New York's Eighth Avenue. I was about to interview mayor Ed Koch, and I was a little nervous . . . nervous enough to drop the notebook I had in my hand. Annoyed, I bent down to pick it up and . . .

Riiiiiiiiiiiiiiiiiiiiiiiip.

My dress pants. The, ah, back seam, if you get my meaning. Right from belt line to crotch.

Luckily, it was New York, so nobody blinked at the sight of the crazy Canuck wearing a white shirt and tie with the tails hanging out. I did the interview, all right, but through the back of my mind a tape loop was playing that said, "Okay, butterball . . . time to lose weight."

I believe it was Mao Zedong (another butterball, now that I think of it) who said: "Even a journey of a thousand miles begins with a single step." I took a lot of single steps. I gave up desserts. Then I gave up midnight snacks. Then mid-afternoon snacks, coffee-break snacks, *all* snacks.

I was still fat.

The battle was joined in earnest. I started giving up things I *really* liked. Things like Crispy Crunch chocolate bars and hamburgers with the works. Even (sob) beer. Pretty soon anything with any alcohol at all was verboten. Goodbye, ice-cold goblet of white wine with the little beads of perspiration running down your lovely flanks; adios, Tequila Sunrises, with that jaunty wedge of lime on the side, so ripe for the sucking; goodbye forever, rum and Cokes, martinis, Manhattans and margaritas. Glenfiddich on the rocks we will not, after all, take a cup of kindness yet. It was fun, but it's over. We're through.

I did it, too. Gave it all up. Booze. Lemon meringue pie. Turtles chocolates. There was just one tiny, lingering problem.

I was still fat.

So I played my trump card: I took up running. Nothing spectacular, you understand. After devoting forty-five years to sloth and dissipation, I wasn't likely to turn into a threat to Ben Johnson overnight. I don't set records, but I sweat, I hurt, I gasp and pant and I get from A to B faster than a speeding garden slug, and that is running to me.

I do not run to hear the cheers of the crowd as I break the tape (fat chance). I do not run to revel in the Zen high of synchronizing muscle and lung and heart.

So why do I run? I do it because I believe that someday I will jiggle off the last of the suet from this bag of flesh and bones and I will be that which I have never been in my life — a thin person.

A sick addiction, I know. Still, it could be worse. I could be Arctic Joe. Now *there's* a running fool. Joe Womersley's a Toronto man who's run just about everywhere you can get to in a pair of running shoes — Alaska, Hawaii, all over the States and Canada.

Where does the "Arctic" in Arctic Joe come from? Oh, he picked that up as organizer of an annual marathon on — wait for it — Baffin Island. Joe's been in charge of it for the past nine years. Last spring, as an extra treat, Arctic Joe organized a team to run a ten-kilometre race around the North Pole. There are now twelve hardy souls in the world who can claim they ran around the world in eighty minutes.

Arctic Joe is one of them, of course. Crazy as a loon, Arctic Joe is. Right now he's in Africa, coping with forty-degree heat and dodging Cape Buffalo as he competes in a 100-k marathon. Mind you, he looks good. Brown as a saddle and well muscled. Clear gaze. Firm handshake. And slim. Did I mention slim?

There's one other thing that Arctic Joe is.

Sixty-two years old.

He's an inspiration for pudgy also-rans like me. I, too, can look as good as Arctic Joe.

I just have to practice for the next fifteen years.

The Last Word on (Hic) coughs

A cough is something you yourself can't help but everyone else does just to torment you.

OGDEN NASH was right, you know. Whenever Your Obedient Correspondent gets a cough, I expect my entire corner of the universe to go on twenty-four-hour medical alert. I want every hospital emergency ward within a 100-mile radius to be notified. I require my local druggist to place himself on round-the-clock standby, ready to use his personal vehicle if necessary to ensure that I have an adequate supply of expectorants, suppressants, antihistamines and nasal sprays. I demand that close friends and even casual acquaintances be available to discuss, drip by drip and honk by honk, my latest symptoms and my ongoing state of agony.

When I, on the other hand, am hale and hearty and someone close by has the bad grace to bark or sneeze or sniffle . . .

I want to kill them.

Last night, at 3:05 A.M., my Sainted Companion and Peerless Partner through the Perils and Pitfalls on the Pathway of Life . . . coughed that most idiotic of all coughs — the hiccough ("hiccup," to us unlettered louts).

And I? Why, I was a veritable Mother Teresa of solicitude and compassion. Right up until the clock's big hand got to the quarter hour and I realized that she was hiccupping louder and more persistently than before.

After considering ear muffs, heavy sedation, a medley of Kate Smith arias at maximum volume and (fleetingly, I swear) asphyxiation by pillow — I gave up, went downstairs and crashed on the sofa. Next morning I showed her my passport photo. Her case of hiccups fairly flew out the window.

194

Hiccups. Is there a stupider affliction that can wrack the human frame? Such a simple malfunction. "A sudden spasm of the diaphragm," my medical dictionary calls it.

And yet so damnably unpredictable. "Most hiccups go away within an hour," says the dictionary. "The hiccup is not serious in itself, but see the doctor if it goes on for more than three hours."

Yes, well, you would have a tough time selling those blandishments to Charlie Osborne. Mr. Osborne is a resident of Aitken, Minnesota, where nothing much of consequence ever seems to happen. But one tiny thing did happen once, back when Charlie was just a young farmhand. He remembers it well.

It was a warm October afternoon and Charlie was slaughtering hogs down by the smokehouse. He had one carcass secured by a chain and was trying to haul it over a tree limb, but it was just too heavy for him. Holding the hog off the ground as best he could, he turned to shout over his shoulder to his wife to come and give him a hand. He opened his mouth to yell "Hilda!"

But instead he hiccupped.

Then he hiccupped again.

And again.

And he's been hiccupping ever since.

An Illinois doctor told him that the strain of lifting the hog carcass probably ruptured a blood vessel going to his brain. Charlie reckons that sounds about as good as any other explanation.

What he does know for sure is that since it happened he's spent more than $40,000 on doctors, evangelists and quack remedies and nothing stops his hiccups. Sometimes they drop off to only one every five or six seconds, other times they climb to a high of forty per minute. But they never stop. Night and day. When he's eating or sleeping or talking or taking a shower, Charlie Osborne has a constant, hated companion.

"I'm used to them now," says Charlie between hiccups, "but I get awful sore. Someday it's gonna kill me, I suppose."

Well, perhaps, but not without a fight. If Charlie's going out, he wants to go with a bang, not a . . . hiccup.

Which is why Charlie made his offer recently: 10,000 U.S. greenbacks to anybody who can cure his hiccups.

And please — don't waste Charlie's time with the obvious old chestnuts like blowing into a paper bag or having someone jump out and scare him. Charlie's tried every hiccup cure your mother ever taught you and several hundred more.

But hey — if you think you have something that'll work, drop him a line. Charlie Osborne, Aitken, Minnesota.

Oh, yes, and you better do it fast.

Charlie Osborne is ninety-three years old.

He's been hiccupping non-stop for the past sixty-five years.

Pillow Thunder

OKAY, 'FESS UP NOW — do you snore?

Naw, me neither — although I'll bet, like me, you're saddled with a companion who insists to the edge of hysteria that sharing a mattress with you is like bedding down with a working chain saw.

It's an odd phenomenon. My own mother swore I snored. So did my brothers and sisters. Now Lynne takes up the same pathetic litany. I'll be lying there in a sound, delicious sleep when suddenly my ribs are rattled by an elbow that would put Gordie Howe to shame.

"Turn over!" she'll growl. "You're snoring!"

No accounting for delusion, I guess.

Funny thing, snoring — funny I mean, to those of us who have never suffered from it. Doctors explain somewhat grandly that it is caused by the vibration of the soft part of the palate, the roof of the mouth and the arch that sweeps down from this behind the tonsils. When a snorer turns on his back, takes a mighty breath and unconsciously put these elements together, he creates a wind instrument that can shiver your timbers, rattle your windows and has caused many a baggy-eyed spouse to ponder the upside of divorce proceedings.

My medical dictionary says that a snore can reach sixty-nine decibels, which puts it just a shade under the noise made by a pneumatic drill.

My newspaper, on the other hand, tells me that it's time to invest in a new medical dictionary. Mine's out of date.

It doesn't know about Mark Hebbard.

Mark's a chap who lives and works and sleeps in a cosy suburb of Richmond, British Columbia. He's surrounded by neighbours who enjoy two out of three of the aforementioned pastimes. They live and work there, but they don't sleep — not when Mark Hebbard's sawing logs. That's because Mark snores. Loudly. Louder in fact, than anyone else in the world. Hebbard is a senior systems analyst when he's awake. When he's asleep he's the terror of his community. He snores so loud that neighbours have called the police. He snores so loud that he could have (but so far hasn't) been arrested for breaking the city noise bylaw. He snores so loud that his wife not only can't sleep in the same room with him — she can't sleep in the same *house*.

Okay. So just how loud does Mark Hebbard snore?

Well, the Canadian Hearing Foundation sent Mark to the University of British Columbia to find out. Doctors and scientists wired him up, put a decibel meter over his head and turned out the lights.

Once he dropped off, Hebbard came in at a constant noise level of eighty-five decibels with several peaks of ninety decibels.

That's five decibels over the maximum permissible noise level under Vancouver law, and only a few decibels below a Black and Decker power saw, a Toro lawn-mower at open throttle, or a heavy metal rock band in full scream.

Mrs. Hebbard says that she has suffered partial hearing loss. "You can imagine what a motorcycle blowing in your ear for fifteen years would do," says her husband. That doesn't surprise me. What does is the fact that there still *is* a Mrs. Hebbard.

Some of Mark's ex-fishing buddies are less loyal. They still remember an overnight salmon fishing trip they took with Mark. Mark warned them of his condition and asked to be bunked with the heaviest snorers on the trip. "I got two of the heaviest snorers," he recalls, "but they couldn't sleep through my snoring. They had to sleep when they were out in the boat fishing."

The good news is, Mark may get asked to go fishing next year. He's just come through an operation that should correct his condition and give Mrs. Hebbard her first decent night's sleep in a decade and a half.

It gives you and me something, too — something to say the next time you-know-who jabs us in the ribs for "allegedly" snoring.

Just ask her how she'd like to spend a night in the sack with Mark Hebbard.

198

Body Graffiti

S O THERE I WAS, stretched out on the beach, lathered up with sunscreen, basting away nicely, just on the edge of drifting off, and the woman next to me says, "Okay, Arthur, what's the story behind the tattoo?"

The . . . what? Oh, the tattoo! Well, you forget you have one, you know — especially when the one you have is small and kind of nondescript and not all that prominent, anyway.

What's the story behind the tattoo? There is a certain edge to the question, as there often is with tattoo queries. The undeclared baggage in this particular inquisition runs along the lines of "How could you be such an idiot?" or "How does it feel to desecrate the temple of your body like that?"

The most interesting thing about sporting a tattoo is the variety of pigeonholes people jimmy you into just for having the thing. Tattoos type you as a rebel, drifter, nonconformist, possible biker/sailor/felon — not to mention dumb. I'm lucky. Mine's small and discreetly tucked away on my upper right arm. I have to take off my shirt before children whimper and strong women swoon.

We humans have been decorating our hides with indelible substances for a long time. Anthropologists have tracked the custom back to 12,000 B.C. Maoris did it, Polynesians did it, Africans and Inuit and Asians did and do it. I walk past a tattoo parlour two or three times a week and I often hear the high-speed whine of the electric tattoo needle. Why do we do it? Not for approval. Tattoos have been denounced and even banned down through the ages by Jews, Muslims and Pope Adrian I. They're not all that hot a draw with lay people, either. Tattoos are a bit like body building. The only people who are remotely impressed are folks who share the affliction.

So why do we get tattoos? I don't know. Why do we smoke? Drive fast? Why does Jerry Lee Lewis comb his hair like that? When I was a kid and even mentioned tattoos, adults came in clouds to convince me I'd be insane to get a tattoo. So of course I went right out and got one. At sixteen, that passes for logic.

Two most common questions from non-tattooed people: number one: were you drunk? Answer: no. But if I had to do it over again I would be. It hurts like hell. Number two: have you ever thought about getting it removed? No, again. That two or three square inches of my skin has had enough abuse for a lifetime. The thought of turning a dermatologist loose on it to sand, burn, freeze or chip away is too revolting to contemplate seriously.

Besides . . . I kind of like the thing. A poor man's coat of arms, somebody once called the tattoo. Well, so be it. Sure beats a business card.

Besides tattoos are not just a moronic male affectation, you know. If you believe the limerick, tattoos can be co-educational and rife with social significance. You know the limerick:

On the chest of a barmaid at Sale
Were tattooed the prices of ale
And on her behind
For the sake of the blind
Was the same information in Braille.

It's a Girl! (Father Expected to Live)

I HAVE BEFORE ME a report in the *Canadian Journal of Anaesthesia* suggesting that fathers should think twice before venturing into the delivery room to get "personally involved" in the birth of their children.

I have several responses to a proposal such as that — two of which are: "No kidding," and "*Now* they tell me."

Where were these experts when I needed them — in the delivery room of St. Joseph's Hospital when my daughter was being born? This, of course, was several years ago. Back in the Age of Mariposa and Woodstock — a Caring, Sharing, Involved and Happening Era when friends in bandanas and denim would say, "Naturally you'll be attending the birth with your wife." "Yup," you would reply. "Oh, sure. You bet. Wouldn't have it any other way."

But of *course* you would share the sacred birth process. Wasn't that what Life Was All About?

Well, yes. Yes, it is. But, friends . . .

It's messy.

It's more than messy — it's mortifying.

Thoreau once said: "Beware of any enterprise that requires new clothes." Black's Corollary reads: "Be extra leery of any enterprise that requires paper slippers and a surgical mask." That's what they dress maternity room Dad voyeurs in — paper slippers and a surgical mask. Then they ask you if you'd mind if a class of student nurses watches the birth.

Now think about this: you are in a room with your wife who is naked and in some considerable distress. The two of you are poised uneasily on the cusp of one of the biggest days of your life.

The authorities want to know if you'd mind if a herd of strangers takes notes. If it happened in your living room, at your office, on the street — anywhere that was even close to your own turf, you would tell the authorities to go pound Sifto, but you are in a strange room full of sundry stainless steel mysteries not to mention tubes and dials and you are wearing paper slippers and a surgical mask. Cowlike, you nod your assent.

Cheer up — this is only the first assault on your dignity. Soon the doctor comes. You can tell he's the doctor because the maternity room staff defers to him. Besides, he's got the rubber gloves on and his surgical mask is regular-issue cloth, not cheap paper like yours.

It's good that you have these clues to the doctor's identity because you'd never figure out who he was from his conversation. He talks like your garage mechanic. He chats about the weather and the Blue Jays and his golf game. He offers his analysis of the current stock market slump. He crows about the gas mileage he gets with his BMW.

And as he talks, this doctor — this *stranger!* — is doing unspeakable things with his hands to your soulmate. But casually! Offhandedly, as it were, like a butcher rearranging the cold cuts in his display cooler.

This is an outrage! A flagrant flouting of everything you hold dear! Are you just gonna stand there like a schnook and allow this to go on? Aren't you going to roar like a bull, rage like a tiger and put these interlopers in their place with your icy, rapier wit?

Wearing paper slippers and a surgical mask? Get serious.

In any case, it will soon get worse. The birthing process is moving along briskly. Your wife is howling and panting and perspiring, pausing only briefly to denounce you, at the top of her lungs, as the source of all pain and evil in the world. You ask her to remember the breathing exercises. She asks you to perform something that is both dexterously demanding and impossible to repeat in a gentle, family-oriented volume such as this.

And now the doctor is brandishing a . . . what is that thing, anyway? A fencing sword? A jackhammer? A jousting lance? No. It is a needle. And he is going to give it to your wife. Oh, my God!!!

That's all I remember. They tell me I hit my head quite a clip on the stirrup on my way to the floor.

Did I mention that we had a beautiful baby girl?
My wife told me all about it in the recovery room.
Mine, not hers.

A Surefire Bet

A LOT OF FOLKS thought my old man was a pretty regular kind of guy, but I knew better. Oh, sure, he *looked* average enough — wife/kids/dog/cat/car/home in the suburbs . . . off to the firm five days a week, snooze on the chesterfield each Sunday afternoon . . . but that was all camouflage . . . protective colouration. In reality my old man was a rogue and a desperado. He carried the evidence in his wallet, tucked in behind his driver's licence, out of sight. He only showed me once, but it raised his status in my eyes till it shimmered on a marble pedestal somewhere between Sir Francis Drake and Rhett Butler. From that moment on, my old man could chit-chat with aristocracy, rub shoulders with royalty, sup with the gods, if he chose to. I was sure of it. After all, he packed . . . an *Irish Sweepstakes ticket.*

Remember them? Exotic-looking slips of parchment they were, all multicolured and crackly. They looked something like a British five-pound note. And best of all, they were illegal.

In Canada, anyway. This was back in Canada's bluestocking period when the thought of a Sunday afternoon baseball game was rankest blasphemy and you had to show your liquor licence and sign your name to buy a bottle of cooking sherry.

Back then I'm not even sure you could *find* the word "gambling" in a Canadian dictionary, but two or three times a year, feral-looking little men in ratty sweaters and shabby peak caps would sidle up to good citizens like my Old Man and, speaking out of the side of their mouths, ask if "You'd like to buy a wee ticket to help build a hospital in Oireland?" That was the moral kicker with the Irish Sweepstakes. It was All for a Good Cause.

The fact that you stood to win $10,000 or $20,000 or $50,000 was practically immaterial.

I don't know how many Irish hospitals ever got built through monies generated by the Irish sweepstakes, but I know a smattering of Canadians won prizes. Their names and sometimes their happy faces appeared in the newspapers from time to time.

Which introduced me to the teeter-totter moral relationship between gambling and the state. It was illegal for Canadians to buy a Sweepstakes ticket but okay for Canadians to win the Sweepstakes.

Curious.

Today, of course, the Canadian government has a much warmer, hands-on relationship with gambling, running the house and skimming the profits as it does from a variety of lotteries and other schemes designed to separate the desperate from their discretionary income. Anybody can buy a lottery ticket along with their quart of 2 per cent down at the corner store.

The pots are bigger but the outlaw thrill is gone.

Personally, I don't gamble — because I'm not particularly lucky and I'm not a pretty loser. Still, from time to time I'm tempted and when I am, I just pull out this piece of advice I have all folded up and tucked behind my driver's licence in my wallet. Mark Twain wrote it. It says: "October. This is one of the peculiarly dangerous months to speculate in. The others are July, January, September, April, November, May, March, June, December, August and February."

I've followed that advice for years, and never lost a bet.

How Much Is That in Plastic?

E VERY SIX MONTHS or so I develop this strange ailment. I start listing noticeably to starboard. I walk down streets as if I'm leaning into a turn on the Indianapolis Speedway. I perch on chairs and stools looking like someone let the air out of one of my buns.

Such symptoms point to one affliction: bloated billfold. It's time once again to administer a high colonic to my wallet.

Credit cards mostly. For some reason people keep sending me credit cards. Maybe they get me confused with *Conrad* Black? I don't know, but usually I'm so pleased to see my name spelled out in gold embossed plastic that I keep the cards — just stuff them into my wallet along with all the others. Then, twice a year on average, I haul out a pair of pinking shears and go through my wallet, separating the chaff from the chaff.

I've got some pips this year. Here's one from a Toronto-based firm that permits me to purchase up to $1,000 worth of mountain-eering equipment.

I have conquered exactly no mountains thus far in my life, and that's a record I fully intend to take to my grave. How the hell did I end up with this card? Here's another one that entitles me to buy groceries in a Florida supermarket chain. I haven't been to Florida in three years!

Here's another that says I'm valued member number 726 of the Canadian Tire Video Club (Fergus, Ontario, chapter) and as such, can rent videocassettes upon presentation of this card.

I happen to know that I can walk in off the street and rent a movie upon presentation of three discs of brass bearing pictures of the loon, so why am I lugging this card around?

Out, out!

I've got a lot of dumb cards to dump, but whenever my personal proliferation of plastic gets me down, I just pause and think of Walter Cavanagh of Santa Clara, California. Walter has more credit cards than I have. As a matter of fact, Walter has more credit cards than you and I and Imelda Marcos have put together. Walter has one thousand . . .

one hundred . . .

and forty-seven credit cards.

And what's more he keeps most of them in a wallet.

A rather special wallet, to be sure — and not one that Walter packs in his hip pocket. It's a custom-made accordion-style job with pockets for 800 cards. Walter could take his wallet to the top of a thirty-storey building and flip it over the side. Unfurled, it would reach all the way to the sidewalk.

Walter has cards that allow him to charge everything from an ice cream cone at Baskin-Robbins to a blackjack game in Reno, Nevada. He applies for at least 100 new cards a month — and gets quite a few of them. Why bother? Glory, partly. His name is already in the *Guinness Book of Records* and *Ripley's Believe It or Not.* But Walter has a target as well. He reckons there are more than 10,000 different charge cards floating around on this continent and he intends to get one of each. "I figure I only have 12 per cent of what's out there. My goal is to get them all."

No doubt Walter's got his eye on the latest credit card to hit the market — fresh from the thermoplastic extrusion machines of Leader Federal Savings and Loan Bank in Memphis, Tennessee: the ElvisCard. No, I'm not making this up. You can now get a black-bordered credit card featuring a rainbow-coloured jukebox and a shot of Elvis, legs akimbo, guitar rampant. The card can bear your name in one corner and the expiry date in the other.

"Give your autograph to Elvis . . . and became part of the legend," says an ad for the card. A mere $36 annually will link your name eternally to the bloated, drug-addicted hillbilly legend.

Be just my luck to receive my very own ElvisCard right after I clean my wallet out. If it happens, I know what I'll do.

Send it right on to Walter Cavanagh.

Better it ends up in his collection than mine.

Auto-mania

L ET'S SUPPOSE AN invasion of killer aliens were to strike our planet tomorrow. Let's suppose these creatures roiled across the surface of the earth, slaughtering humans by the hundreds of thousands, devouring millions of tons of vital, irreplaceable earthly fluids, infesting thousands of square miles of prime land and reducing our largest cities to a shrieking, stinking paralysis by sheer force of numbers.

What do you suppose we would call a catastrophe like that?

A plague? Monsters from Outer Space? The Creatures That Took over the Earth?

We already have that catastrophe. And we've got a name for it, as well.

We call it the automobile.

We don't consider the car to be a catastrophe, of course — far from it. We (with a helpful nudge from the Detroit Big-Three Ad Copywriters) look on cars as sexual turn-ons and fashion statements, status symbols and pleasure wagons.

But the old family chariot is a bit more than that. You have to have a grudging respect for any terrestrial phenomenon that, without declaring war, has managed to kill more North Americans than all the bombs of the First and Second World Wars put together.

By a long shot — more than two million of us have perished behind the wheels and under the bumpers of cars. More than six million people on this continent have been crippled for life by car accidents.

Imagine the entire population of British Columbia, Alberta and

208

Saskatchewan in wheelchairs, body casts or on life-support systems — that's an automotive legacy the glossy TV ads don't talk about.

Picture the entire citizenry of Calgary, Vancouver and St. John's pushing up marble — that's another.

Cars may be killing us in other ways, as well: each vehicle spews out about a ton of noxious air pollutants annually. And who could put a dollar figure on the amount of land we devote to the beasts in the form of parking lots, freeways, highways, byways and cloverleafs? Insurance agents and auto-repair shops grow sleek and fat on our auto addiction. Oil-company executives have a swell time in the boardroom inventing new ways to separate car owners from their money. The people want unleaded gas, do they? Jolly good — we'll stop putting lead in the gas, but we'll charge them more for it! What fun!

The money we lavish on cars is scarcely credible. Do you know how much $1 billion is? It is more than half the annual budget of some Canadian provinces. If you counted out a hundred loonies a minute for eight hours a day, five days a week, it would take you eighty years to reach $1 billion.

One billion dollars also represents the total of unpaid traffic tickets in New York City for one calendar year.

For some of us, car love has passed over the line into car obsession. A couple of years ago, a California woman was buried propped up behind the wheel of her favourite Ferrari, in accordance with her wishes.

Bad enough to worship cars — in Yugoslavia you can worship *before* them. There's a small-town Yugoslavian priest who ushers in summer each year by blessing thousands of cars. Parishioners (carishioners?) all park reverently for the occasion in front of a special mobile altar made of two Fiats. And in New York there's a woman who took her Cadillac to an altar. Not to worship — to wed. Yes, she married it, to the musical strains of "The Wedding March" — tooted out on car horns, of course.

And finally, there is Carhenge. Carhenge is an American copy of Britain's Stonehenge, rising on the shoulder of U.S. Interstate 385 just outside Alliance, Nebraska — except it's made of — you guessed it — junk cars. Carl Reinders, the man responsible for Carhenge, says, "If Stonehenge has some purpose, then I think

Carhenge has some purpose." Well, don't try to sell that to a Druid, Carl. Still, you have to wonder what some archaeologist stumbling across Carhenge, say a hundred years from now, would make of twenty-two rusting cars all standing on their hoods.

Come to think of it, he might see our obsessive auto-eroticism a whole lot clearer than we do ourselves.

Lawn Order

NEXT TIME I RUN into a cultural anthropologist, I'm going to drag him or her off to a quiet corner somewhere and beg for an explanation of the Lawn Cult.

You know the Lawn Cult. You're probably a disciple yourself. Most of us are. We're the people who spend money, time and muscle power to find new and ever more expensive ways to make our lawns grow faster so that we can spend ever-increasing amounts of money, time and muscle power cutting them.

What's with lawns, anyway? Lawns are not oats or barley or canola. You can't bale them or stook them or turn them into wheat sheaves. We don't get beautiful flowers or succulent fruit from the lawn. A lawn is just . . . green. If you're *lucky*, it's green. Sometimes it's brown or scabby or be-zitted with dandelions and crab grass, which calls for massive new transfusions of money, hours and sweat to get it back to plain old green again.

Ever looked at a single grass plant? Homeliest bit of handiwork in the entire botannical catalogue. Go pull one out of your lawn, check it out. It's okay — you can afford it. There are about 850 plants in every square foot of average lawn. Plucking one out isn't going to make any difference. Hold the spindly little spike of greenery up to the light. Not exactly a towering redwood or a tropical orchid, is it? Not the sort of thing you'd think would have the power to obsess grown humans and gobble up their week-ends.

But it does. I know a guy who spends his Sunday afternoons crawling around his lawn on his hands and knees with a paring knife playing search and destroy with insurgent weed species. I don't have the comparable Canadian figures, but according to a brochure from the Lawn Institute (Yes, Virginia, there is a Lawn Institute) Americans spend $25 billion a year catering to their lawns.

And all for what? To encourage a decidedly mundane, utterly unproductive species of vegetation to sprout, then to behead it, practically the instant it sticks its little growing tip out of the ground. Why this passion for not just lawns but *shorn* lawns? Lawns that look like the top of the head of a Marine Corps rookie?

I once heard that we cut our lawns to show our neighbours how rich we are. It's a habit that goes back to medieval times when wealthy folks were the ones who had sheep and cattle . . . and you could tell where *they* lived because the grass was grazed short by their livestock. Nowadays, of course, we wouldn't allow live-stock on our lawn. They'd ruin it.

There was a poignant little news story in the paper this week about a fellow who was charged with impaired driving in down-town Dartmouth, Nova Scotia. He was piloting a riding lawn-mower. Police said no one was injured but a couple of city lawns were unexpectedly mowed. Sounds to me like a plaintive cry for help from someone who's gone on one to many missions cutting swathes with his Toro in the noonday sun. I think we'll be seeing a lot more of that, as Lawn Cult Burnout spreads. I hope we see some of it in my neighbourhood. Soon. My lawn is open to being unexpectedly mowed by anyone who feels the urge.

Two Cheers for the Post Office

*If any Gentlemen, Merchants, or others, wants to
send any Letters to any Foreign Port, they may
depend on having their Letters carefully deliver'd
to the Captain of the first Vessel bound for the Place
to which their Letters are directed, by paying One
Penny per Letter to said Office.*

THEIR HUMBLE SERVANT,
BENJAMIN LEIGH

T HE ABOVE AD APPEARED in the *Halifax Gazette* on April 27,
1754 — the first evidence of what would grow to become
Canada Post.

And unless I miss my guess, by April 28, 1754, disgruntled
colonialists were swapping the first anti-post-office jokes.

Ah, the post office. It's the brunt of more one-liners than
telephone operators, airline food and Jewish mothers-in-law combined. Why do Canadians love to hate the post office so?

Part of it is performance, of course — or lack of it. Canada Post
is forever getting shot in its corporate foot by the fatuous clowns
who work there — on both sides of the picket fence.

Remember the famous quote from the lips of Jean-Claude
Parrot, president of the Canadian Union of Postal Workers, back
in 1978? His union had just been ordered by court injunction to go
back to work. Mr. Parrot faced the nation via the TV cameras and
snarled, "You want to mail a letter? Just try it."

That's the kind of talk that tax-paying citizens of a democracy
are really keen to hear.

But it wasn't just the labour side of Canada Post that got the nation's
goat. André Ouellette, postmaster-general, once blandly told the

Globe and Mail, "I can't accept that businessmen have to rely on the post office to make a living. If they do, they better find other ways."

What planet do these people *live* on?

Sometimes the post office seems to be engaged in one long banana-skin slide, stumbling and careering from Chaplinesque gaffe to Three Stooges pratfall.

It introduces, with great fanfare, Supermailboxes.

They don't work and everybody hates them.

It announces, in a series of slick and expensive newspaper ads "new streamlining procedures to improve efficiency." First thing it does is close a whole clutch of small-town post offices, throwing people out of work and shattering a time-honoured rural tradition.

And how do citizens fight back? With jokes, of course.

"Know how to become postmaster-general? Make the prime minister very, very angry."

"It now costs forty cents to mail a letter. Fifteen cents for delivery; twenty-five cents for storage."

Then there's Allen Fotheringham's wicked solution: "It could be ordered that post office workers receive their cheques by mail."

But you know, when all is said and done, I think maybe we give the post office a bit of a bum rap. Sure, it's inefficient — but no more than the phone company or Ottawa or those idiots who keep billing you for magazines you never received and don't want. We Canucks will line up at supermarket checkouts or sit in doctors' offices like good little sheep for hours with nary a bleat of protest, but let three people get in front of us at the stamp wicket and we start rummaging around for tar and feathers.

Pity the poor posties — even when they win they lose. Did you read about that Ontario farmer who received a letter last month with a King George V stamp on it? It had the stamp because it was mailed in 1931. "Must have got stuck behind some machinery," an official explained. Har har. Big laugh on the post office for losing a letter for sixty years.

But the really remarkable thing is that the posties delivered the letter. Just as they're supposed to. Even though they knew they were in for a merciless razzing.

That's class. Not First Class, but class.

I say, Two Cheers for the Post Office!

I'd give 'em all three, but they have to lose something for lousy dusting.

We're Eating Too Fast

THERE'S A STORY in the local paper about a teenage French exchange student who's spent the past ten months living here in Canada, in my hometown, as a matter of fact. He told the reporter in his somewhat teetery English that it's been quite an experience for him. He's visited New York and climbed the Empire State Building; he's gone to northern Ontario and fished for walleye and pike; he's seen the sights of Toronto — the CN Tower, Ontario Place. But what, asked the reporter, was the overall impression he would take back with him to France?

"Food," said the French student. "You eat a lot of greasy food. There are only a few McDonalds in France."

Isn't it odd that a visitor from France will remember our country not as a land of wilderness or wheatfields or mountains or Mounties but as a land of Golden Arches — not to mention Harveys and Wendys and Tasty Freezes and Taco Bells? We Canadians — we North Americans — like to feed on the fly. And that means fast food — the faster the better.

Who can wait for messy, time-consuming ancient customs like simmering, braising, grilling, stewing? Microwave it till it stops moving, throw it on a bun and pass the mustard. You want taste? Suck a breath mint.

And our junk food is getting . . . junkier. Have you discovered Sea Pasta yet? It's the latest thing in the fast fish-food business. Sea Pasta comes as a *glop* in a pasta shell. The glop consists of wheat flour, water, celery, onion, sugar, cornstarch, sorbital, salt, potato starch, natural and artificial flavours, egg white, artificial colour, vegetable oil, hydrolized animal protein, monosodium glutamate,

216

sodium pyrophosphate, sodium tripolyphosphate, glyceril mono-stearate — oh, yes, and some fish, too.

Have you heard the latest thrust of Coca-Cola's advertising plans? They want to penetrate the *breakfast* market. Forget prune, apple or orange juice — let's all wash down our sugar-frosted Captain Crunchies with a fizzy glass of Coke Classic.

Our love affair with junk food doesn't make any sense — but what love affair ever did? The famous baseball player (and junk-food junkie) Yogi Berra had the right attitude. The waitress in his favourite pizza parlour asked him if he wanted his pizza cut in four slices or eight. "Better make it four," decided the Yogi. "I don't think I could eat eight."

A difficult attitude to explain to the French who treat food with the love and respect we Canadians reserve for trophy-size muskies and Stanley Cup champions.

Still, I'm not so sure about what awaits that French exchange student when he goes back home. Fast-food mania is a worldwide infestation and no respecter of borders. I have a hunch he'll find more than a few burger joints and taco takeouts when he gets back to La Belle France.

An American senator from California had that experience when he visited his ancestral homeland of Japan a few years back. "There are more than a hundred fast-food eating places over there," moaned Senator S. I. Hayakawa. "That seems a terrible price to pay for Pearl Harbor."

Run for Your Life! They're Playing Conway Twitty!

If I had to choose between music and sex, I would pause a long time.

DONALD BARTHELME

W ELL, I DARESAY the U.S. novelist somewhat overstates the case for most of us, but maybe not. Perhaps music really is that important to most people. I only know that it's not for me.

I don't know who left out what in the fetal fondue my mom and dad whipped up. All I know is I came out of it with a couple of conspicuous gaps in my chromosomal repertoire — viz: the genes responsible for manufacturing head hair and music appreciation.

Which is not to say that I don't like music — I do. Everything from Fats Waller to Gustav Mahler; from Jascha Heifetz to Harmonica Jake. I like it fine. I just don't *love* it, is all. Other folks are more sensitive. I have a friend who can't hear more than a dozen bars of Beethoven without crying. The Syrian general Nicator fainted at the sound of a flute.

I once demonstrated all the symptoms of seasickness after listening to an accordion band at a polka party, but I don't think that counts.

I can identify with what the English writer George Eliot had to say on the subject. "Music," wrote Eliot, "sweeps by me like a messenger carrying a message that is not for me."

It was even harder for Eliot, of course. She lived in the nineteenth century — which means she went through her entire life without once hearing a Barry Manilow ballad.

Maybe that's our problem. Maybe we've rotted out our musical molars on a diet of melodic junk food — too much Manilow and

218

Madonna, an overdose of doo-wops from Little Martha and the VibeTones.

Come to think of it, why are we subjected to such cruddy music so much of the time? Why is the hit parade constantly clogged with vapid tunes warbled by tiny talents like Tiffany, for crying out loud? Who ever voted for the syrupy treacle of Muzak? Wouldn't it be great to walk into a mall or an elevator and hear Ella Fitzgerald or Moe Koffman or Liona Boyd coming over the public address system?

But perhaps that's the whole point of gonadless music. Maybe it's a kind of aural narcotic to keep the workers drowsy and the shoppers grazing peacefully. Music as a crowd-control agent? Why not? Officials of the Canadian National Exhibition in Toronto have a problem with teenage hooligans who congregate in the midway, drawn like moths to the loud rock music that's played there. Too often the louts work themselves into a frenzy and go on a rampage, trashing stalls and starting fights.

One CNE official has proposed a surefire, hassle-free way of making the rockers disperse. "Play country music over the public address system," he says. "It's the only music they really hate."

Interesting idea — music as crowd repellent. If that works, maybe we would twig to the notion of using music as a crowd attractant, a psychic balm to bring people together and make them feel good—which, if I'm not mistaken, is the whole point of music.

They're already doing it in other parts of the world. In the subways of New York and Boston, passengers often come upon the incongruous sight of a string quartet or a woodwind ensemble playing classical music on the platform. It's a service provided by the transit authorities in an attempt to soothe the frayed nerves of commuters.

How does the travelling public like it? "Beautiful," said one damp-eyed straphanger who had stopped to listen to a brass quintet deep in the bowels of Grand Central Station. "If they had a little more music, you'd feel more comfortable down here. People wouldn't be so mean."

Sounds to me like an idea that's too good to leave in the subways. Bring it out of the American underground, I say.

And since we'll never get a chance to vote on Free Trade, let's at least make sure that the idea of Good Music in the Streets is high on our list of imports.

Tasty, but Is It Art?

I SEE THE MONTREAL Art World has worked itself up into a lather. The "to-do" has to do with a huge gash in a painting that was on display in a special exhibition at Montreal's Museum of Contemporary Art.

The painting is an abstract by the artist Sigmar Polke. It now looks as if it's been love-tapped by Freddie Kreuger. A ragged five-inch-by-three-inch rip runs right across the centre of the canvas.

The owner of the painting was less upset about the damage than she was about the cavalier response of the curators. Wealthy collector Lonti Ebers has charged the museum with "unprofessionalism and blatant contempt." She claims they "deliberately withheld information" about the rip "until a shocking seventeen days after the discovery of the damage."

Well, I hesitate to dip my philistine toe into the boiling waters of an Art controversy, but I think I know what the problem is here.

I don't believe that the folks at the Museum of Contemporary Art are guilty of unprofessionalism or contempt. I doubt that they were trying to cover up the damage or mislead the owner.

My guess is, they didn't know whether or not the gash was supposed to be part of the painting.

It's no longer easy for serious and committed art lovers to understand the totality of an artistic statement. Used to be that painters could be relied on to slap down canvasses covered with cows or mountains or Naked Majas. An art connoisseur or a curator could hold it out at arm's length, squint and say, "That's a damned fine cow!" or "Now, this Maja is much more Naked than his early Naked Majas."

Chaps like Renoir, Goya, Rembrandt and Velasquez routinely delivered paintings of sunsets and nymphets, battle scenes and dotty monarchs that even a child could recognize, if not entirely appreciate.

Then the Dadaists and Cubists rode into town. Pretty soon Georges Braque was turning out paintings that looked as if they'd been painted on glass, then shattered with a brick. Picasso introduced us to painted characters that appeared as cartoon mutants with extra breasts and both eyes on the same side of their faces, like Dover soles.

And that was merely the beginning.

Nowadays painters turn out works with murky titles like *Study #398* or *Symbiosis/Dodge Galaxy*.

It's difficult to sound intelligent when you're gazing at a canvas that looks as if it fell off the truck face down in a muddy parking lot.

And more than a few people have been fooled. Back in 1961, the Museum of Modern Art in New York reverently unveiled a painting called *Le Bâteau* by famous French expressionist Henri Matisse. It hung in the gallery for forty-six days, drawing adoring crowds and ecstatic reviews until someone murmured, "Errr, isn't that . . . upside down?"

It was.

I imagine the museum staff was almost as embarrassed as Edward Brzezinski not long ago. Brzezinski, a New York artist himself, had wandered into a SoHo gallery featuring an exhibition of work by sculptor Robert Gober.

"Trite stuff," Brzezinski said to himself as he ambled through the exhibits. "Working-class kitsch. Predictable. Derivative. At least they laid on some hors d'oeuvres."

And Brzezinski reached out to an open bag of doughnuts, snagged one and scarfed it down.

Which is when the gallery owner descended upon him, shrieking and swearing. Brzezinski, hiccupped the owner, had just desecrated an original Robert Gober sculpture, pricetagged at $8,000.

It's difficult to say which bothered Edward Brzezinski more —

the knowledge that as an art connoisseur, he'd blown it, or the fact that he was carrying a doughnut treated with an industrial plastic preservative in his belly.

Whatever, eyewitnesses report that Brzezinski definitely had a glazed look about him.

That's Gold in Them Thar Poems

T HE OTHER DAY when I was padding and browsing through a bookstore in downtown Toronto, it suddenly occurred to me that somebody was missing.

I checked the Poetry Section. Wasn't there. Checked the Canadiana section. Wasn't there, either. I asked the clerk, and she mouthed those words that must haunt the dreams of authors everywhere:

"Service? Service . . . what sort of things does he write?"

Did write ma'am . . . and it was poetry. Canadian poetry. Although a lot of bigdomes and greybeards dismiss the writing of the bank clerk from Kamloops as mere doggerel.

Well, perhaps he wasn't Keats or Yeats or even Irving Layton, but on some subjects, I don't know anybody who wrote better than Robert Service.

For instance . . . gold.

Did anybody ever capture the strange hypnosis of gold fever better than Service, when he wrote:

There are strange things done in the midnight sun
By the men who moil for gold.

Service lived in the Klondike during the Gold Rush, and he saw what it did to men and women and the Yukon. But then, lust for gold has written quite a few chapters of Canadian history and not always with the help of Robert Service. Timmins and Kirkland Lake, El Dorado, Red Lake . . . even the town of Flin Flon, Manitoba. It got its name from a wandering gold prospector, who happened to be reading a dime-store novel in which the hero, one professor Josiah Flintabbety Flonatin, finds a sunless city, with gold lying in the streets.

Legend has it that gold in the Flin Flon area was found by that same prospector throwing his pick at a whiskeyjack. The pick missed, struck a lichen-covered rock, scraping the lichen away to reveal . . . you guessed it. The yellow stuff of who knows how many dreams.

And the dreaming continues. There's a gold rush of sorts going on right now. Any day, you could receive a phone call from somebody offering to sell you a pile of dirt for a mere $5,000 U.S.

Mind you, you get a lot of dirt for that — about a hundred tons. And the investor will guarantee — stone guarantee — that that dirt pile contains at least twenty ounces of gold. Maybe hundreds of ounces. Well . . . twenty ounces of gold for $5,000 with gold trading up over the $400 mark — that's a deal. Or it would be, if the gold was recoverable. It's not. It's in the form of microscopic flakes. You'd find more gold by going to the outskirts of Flin Flon and throwing prospecting picks at whiskeyjacks. The dirt-pile gold rush is a fraud and a scam, but that hasn't stopped investors from lining up to throw their money away — so far, to the tune of more than a quarter of a million dollars. The lure of the gold.

What was it Service wrote?

I wanted the gold and I sought it,
I scrabbled and mucked like a slave.
Was it famine or scurvy — I fought it.
I hurled my youth into a grave.
I wanted the gold and I got it.
Came out with a fortune last fall.
Yet somehow life's not what I thought it.
And somehow the gold isn't all.

Maybe if those investors had read their Service, they'd have saved their money.

Have a Cheroot, Rudyard?

I'VE BEEN SITTING here, totting up my physical frailties. Plotting a mental graph of my various muscular aches, tonguing the gaps between my teeth, gaps that used not to be there, monitoring that curious little sonar ping I feel in my chest from time to time . . . and wondering exactly when this all began to happen to me. Middle age, I mean. It's not as if you wake up one morning to skyrockets, orchestral music and a large ethereal voice saying, "Congratulations, Arthur Black . . . you've arrived!" You don't get a bar mitzvah or a stag party for Middle Age. Nope, one moment you're boiling along there with the rest of the crowd, wassailing with the best of them, then suddenly the train pulls out, the crowd dissipates and you find yourself standing on the platform of a rather shabby-looking station you'd never noticed before.

Middle Age. Closest I can get to that precise instant when the floor dropped away was that moment when I realized in my heart that the Montreal Canadiens coach was *not* going to call.

Make no mistake about my hockey skills. I couldn't put a puck in the net with a snow shovel, I hold my stick like a crutch and I skate on my ankles, using the blades as outriggers, but like all Canadian lads I just assumed there was an immense reservoir of raw talent lying dormant within, and some eagle-eyed NHL scout would spot it and sign me. He didn't . . . and one day it dawned on me that quite aside from being no good, I was too old to play pro hockey.

That's what I think Middle Age is — the realization that there are some things you just aren't going to get to do this go-round.

Things like . . . well, ride the Orient Express. I always dreamed that one day I would board that fabled train in some rosy Parisian dawn and ride her all the way to Istanbul. I won't. We both hit middle age, and only I survived. They yanked the Orient Express off the tracks. Oh, she's been quasi-resurrected for a couple of little tourist toots. But she doesn't leave from Paris, she leaves from Boulogne and she doesn't run to Istanbul, her final destination is Vienna. Well, that's hardly the Orient, is it? That's like Torontonians who tell you they have a cottage "up north" when they mean Lake Simcoe.

The other institution that slammed its door in my face before I could sample it was Raffles. I always wanted to at least have a drink at Raffles, and now I never will. The 103-year-old Singapore hotel, where Kipling and Conrad, Coward and Maugham wrote and stayed, has taken its last guest. It is being demolished.

Someday Disneyland will no doubt feature a new exhibit — it'll be a plastic train that runs through plastic reconstructions of Baghdad, Constantinople and Istanbul. Orient Express World they will call it, and Mickey, Minnie and Goofy will serve non-alcoholic drinks with paper umbrellas in them and welcome you at the end of the line to Raffles World, a plastic hotel where all the chambermaids look like Snow White and Huey, Dewey and Louie take your bags.

Well, I won't be riding. Or signing in. I'll be holding out in the bar at the Terminal Lounge. That's me in the white linen suit, with the panama hat and the Malacca cane, smoking a cheroot, right between Rudyard Kipling and Somerset Maugham.

Can I get you something? Singapore Sling?

Neither Shy Nor Retiring

YOU KNOW WHAT makes me feel old? Whenever I hear anybody talking about retirement, that's what. Retirement. What a strange concept. "Well, if everyone will excuse me I think I'll stop doing what I've been doing for forty-five years and 'retire' for the rest of my life . . ."

But I guess it nails us all sooner or later. Down in Florida right now, a somewhat more off-the-wall development in the retirement scene is unfolding — one that's bound to make anybody who lived through the sixties feel as if he's ready for the antique shelf.

I refer to the plans of an organization called Love of Rock and Roll Inc. in Seminole, Florida. L of R and R is trying to raise $27 million to build a retirement home for superannuated . . . rock and roll stars — well, not stars — meteors, if you will. Performers who've faded from the limelight and are a little too long of tooth and arthritic of pelvis to stage a comeback.

The Rock and Roll Haven will boast features you don't often find in retirement homes, such as a recording studio and a bandstand where venerable rockers can get together and reminisce harmonically.

I guess Cher had a couple of rock 'n' roll hits way back when, didn't she? Imagine if she ever fell on hard times and fetched up at the door of the Rock and Roll retirement home? Then every Saturday night the residents could get together and sing a toothless chorus of "Ol' Rockin' Cher's Got Me . . ."

But never mind — there's an even stranger retirement home about 1,500 miles due west of Seminole, Florida, across the Gulf of Mexico. It's on the grounds of the Southwest Foundation for Biomedical Research in San Antonio, Texas. There are eighty residents in this retirement home. They get free medical care and exercise facilities, and they get to watch a lot of television and eat a lot of fruit.

Which we assume suits them just fine. We *have* to assume that because not one of the eighty residents speaks English. They are all . . . chimpanzees.

These chimps have been used in medical research — chiefly in the fields of hepatitis and AIDS. They're all healthy, but because of what they've been exposed to, they can't be used for any future testing. Which is a problem because chimps usually live about forty-five years and these guys are all teenagers.

Well, not such a problem as it turns out, because somebody at the Biomedical Research Foundation has a heart. These chimps have been fitted with golden parachutes. They have their own condo, their own colour television sets, and thanks to the drug companies who finance the foundation, a $3 million nest egg to cover the rent, pay for the gardener and keep them in bananas for at least the next three or four decades.

Those chimps are retired. And on them it looks good. Puts me in mind of a story about ex U.S. president Calvin Coolidge. Soon after he left office, Coolidge had to fill out a form to join a club. In the space marked Occupation, Coolidge wrote "Retired." The next space read "Remarks." Cool Cal thought for a bit and then scribbled: "Glad of it."

Hat-napped

WELL, IT WAS A PRETTY good week for me. Sold my hat. No, I'm serious. You know the one? That salt-and-pepper cloth cap I sported for the past millennium or so? I unloaded it.

Way it happened, I was back in my hometown to take part in a radiothon fundraiser for the Thunder Bay Symphony Orchestra. You know, where you hijack the airwaves and ask people to phone in their pledges. Well, we hit a stretch of the doldrums there for about twenty minutes where nobody was phoning in, and we wondered what we could do to inject a little juice into the proceedings. "Why don't we auction off Black's hat?" somebody said. I took the moth-eaten old thing off my head, looked at it and said, "Sure, why don't we?" So we did. Told listeners to phone in their bids. Got a nibble right away. Somebody phoned in and offered $25. Couple of minutes later, somebody'd upped it to $35. Well, all right, I thought to myself.

That's when one of the pledge-takers came up to the stage and said in a small, strangled voice, "I think you can close off the bidding now. Somebody's just offered to buy your hat . . . for $1,000."

It was true! A woman who insisted on remaining anonymous had made a bid of $1,000.

Well, I mean, have you seen that hat? Up close? Put it this way. If my hat was a car and Richard Nixon was a used-car salesman, he wouldn't have it on his lot. I'll tell you how baffed it is. Charlie Farquharson saw it on my head once and offered to trade even-steven. That hat was a wreck. The lining's kinda torn and there's a little spray of aluminum paint on the brim from the time I wore it while I was touching up the handlebars on my bike. There's a patch near the back that looks like a vermilion-coloured map of Labrador — that's a sherry stain that goes back to a swanky soirée the CBC Suits on Bay Street threw last spring. And there's a long burn mark right next to it that was incurred when the hat did double duty as a pot holder at a lobster barbecue on the beach near Souris, PEI, a couple of summers back.

Somebody paid 1,000 bucks for that. Sheesh.

I mean it's not as if I needed the hat. I've got a closet full of hats. I've got a Calgary Stetson, a Trois-Rivières toque.

I've got Fedoras, panamas, an Australian bushman's snap brim. I've got a beret in case I ever have a book launching in Nice or Barcelona, for crying out loud. I'm covered for hats. Most of them have never even been worn. Amazing how maudlin people can get over something as silly as a hat, though. After I sold the thing and was sitting there bare (okay, bald) headed, kind of chortling over the deal, a woman came out of the crowd and handed me a card. The card read, "In Deepest Sympathy. Our thoughts are with you in this your moment of loss." And underneath the message the woman had written in ball-point: "Your loss has made us all quite blue. Because that hat was part of you."

That old thing? Listen, the only good thing I can tell you about that hat is that it never, in my travels through all ten provinces, down the Klondike River in a canoe, through I don't know how many bush-plane rides, several bus-chasing sprints, a couple of full gallops on horseback, a torrential downpour in the Dominican Republic and two complete circuits of the Wild Mouse at the CNE, it never blew off my head. It never blew off because . . . it fitted my head. Perfectly.

Do you suppose she'd take $1,100 if I threw in a Greek fisherman's cap?

Junk Mail Burns Me Up — and Vice Versa

I F YOU DEEM YOURSELF to be a person of an exquisitely sensitive nature . . . better you should turn the page right now. If you see a little old lady or anyone with a heart condition perusing this page, gently but firmly remove the book from his or her grasp and suggest a stroll, or perhaps some television. This space is about to erupt with two very foul four-letter words . . . a double-barrelled expletive that is perhaps the filthiest in the entire English language. Are you ready?

Junk Mail.

There. I said it and I'm glad I said it, but having said it . . . what to do about it? If you are an average North American man, woman or child, you receive 614 pieces of mail each year — 230 pieces of which you did not ask for, expect, or in fact want.

The 230 pieces were what the post office likes to call "complimentary, pre-approved direct-mail items" — junk mail to you, me and the poor, hernia-courting letter carrier who has to lug them from door to door.

Near as I can figure, there are only two really tough questions in the whole junk mail problem. One is, How did they get my name?

The second is, How do I get revenge?

The answer to the first question is storks. I reckon that thanks to the Pill, storks, which used to work around the clock depositing babies under cabbage leaves, are now forced to moonlight for a living. Instead of delivering our kids they deliver our names to the large mail-order houses.

As for the second problem — getting revenge — that's tougher. I've tried various gambits over the years. For a few weeks I assiduously packed up my unwanted mail and sent it back to the companies it came from, postage due. But all that earned me was

231

a bad bout of writer's cramp and some very withering glares from the folks at the post office.

Why not just throw it into a Glad bag and leave it out with the trash each week? Well, that gets it off my coffee table, all right, but it's not exactly revenge, is it? Besides, it's an environmental copout. Our landfill sites are already choked to overflowing with dead refrigerators, rusty bedsprings and old car tires. They don't need my mounds and moguls of postal pollution piled on top.

I fought a losing battle with my junk mail for years, until one day my eye fell on a newspaper photograph of some guy's mailbox in Colorado.

It's kind of electric when you stumble across a kindred spirit. The owner of this mailbox clearly was one. Like you and me, he'd had his fill of junk mail. Like you and me, he felt an urge to strike back, and he did.

His mailbox was a horizontal garbage can welded to a post.

Cute . . . but ultimately ineffectual. It made a statement but it failed to kick the Junk Mailers where it hurts.

On the other hand, it did give me an idea. I immediately went out and bought the best-looking tin garbage can my plastic charge card could buy.

But I didn't weld it to a post. Instead I got out some black paint, an artist's paintbrush and in a shaky attempt at Old Gothic Script, I painstakingly lettered a single word on the side of the can:

KINDLING

The can sits beside my tiny pot-bellied stove even as I type, and when I'm finished typing I will go down to my mailbox, bring back the day's offering and sort it over the can. Everything I actually want to read goes to one side, the rest of it gets deep-sixed right into the galvanized maw.

If the junk mailers struck me from their lists tomorrow I'd still have enough kindling to carry me well into spring.

Try it! Get yourself a little acorn stove — or hell, just fire up the hibachi! The knowledge that junk mail is helping to heat your home is enough in itself to make you feel warm all over.

Go ahead! Burn those phony travel brochures, those "free for a limited time only" offers, those sweepstakes entries and life-insurance applications, those flyers, those leaflets, those old books . . .

Wait a minute.

Not the books. No, I was just kidding. It was a slip of the tongue. Now *hold it! That's not funny!* Look, there are some very good stories inside! *Stop that! You're creasing my dust jacket!* Mmmmmmpppphhhhhh . . .